THE

FISHING FANATIC

THE
FISHING
FANATIC

Quotes and Brags from
Experts and Wags

**Edited and with an introduction
by Damian R. Rubino**

THE LYONS PRESS
Guilford, Connecticut
An imprint of The Globe Pequot Press

Introduction and text order copyright © 2007 by Damian Rubino

The Lyons Press is an imprint of The Globe Pequot Press

10 9 8 7 6 5 4 3 2 1

Printed in the United States of America

Designed by Nancy Freeborn/Freeborn Design

ISBN: 978-1-59228-992-9

Library of Congress Cataloging-in-Publication Data is available
on file.

DEDICATION

I dedicate this book to all my fishing buddies, especially Jeff, Joel, my brothers Greg and Matt, and to fishing fanatics the world over. May you always fish in clearest pools—with a fair breeze at your back—and catch things extraordinary, be they fish or memories of time well spent in Nature.

I would like to acknowledge the unfailing help of my editor, Holly Rubino, whose guidance and suggestions made this work a reality. You are the best. And to all the folks at the Lyons Press, thank you one and all.

CONTENTS

INTRODUCTION

Who is a fishing fanatic? Is it the fly fisherman or woman dressed in L. L. Bean clothes and sporting Orvis-made equipment that all together cost as much as a new pickup in 1979? Is it Quint from *Jaws*, "I'll catch your shark for $5,000 but kill 'im for $10," the modern-day Ahab? Is it the tournament boys, rigged up with more hi-tech equipment than the first Apollo mission to the moon? It is the little kid, with a cane pole, cork bobber, and coffee can of red wigglers dunking a line in a nearby farm pond to catch sunfish? Yes, yes, yes, and yes. A fanatic can be all of these and more. A fanatic is you, me, your dad, mom, granddad, brother, sister. This little book is here to celebrate everyone and the memorable things fanatics like you and me have said throughout the ages.

My own earliest recollection of fishing is digging worms at the edge of "The Brook" with Johnny

Chapman. His left hand only had four fingers on account of the fact that he left the pinkie attached to the ladder rack on his dad's truck when he jumped off it a few years back. I went with him on more than one occasion when I was five or so years old to drown worms and to try to catch rainbow trout at a little brook that ran out of Perkins Pond. The pond is now just a swampy area filled with cat-o'-nine-tails and the brook just a trickle, maybe, but those trips up the street from my boyhood home served to hook me on a sport that still manages to delight and confound me to this very day.

Do you have a Johnny Chapman? A fishing muse? Someone who set you on the path of "quietness, and virtue, and Angling" (Izaak Walton)? If so, give this book to that special someone. Or are you the fishing Yoda for a bass-bustin' Luke Skywalker? Have you inspired someone to take up rod and reel and head out for the nearest water? If this be true, keep it for yourself and three cheers to he or she who has inspired the next Bill Dance or Steve Raymond. The world needs more of these types, both inspirers and inspirees. In a word, fanatics.

The quotes collected in this book spring from the thoughts of wise men and fools, poets and rogues, from the Bard himself to bad boy Bassmaster Mike Iaconelli, the self-described "freaky, tattooed angler from South Jersey," and everyone in between. The inspiration to collect them came from my editor/wife and my own love of words and fishing. These quotes are small truths, uttered in moments of candor and re-alization that sometimes fishing ain't just fishing—it can also be a metaphor for life. I've tried to select as great a variety of quotes as possible, in order to demonstrate the endless ways in which fishing is done and Monday-morning quarterbacked. I want to show the variety of people who have practiced the art of fishing and then commented upon it, spanning hundreds of years and millions of words. But my point and the authors' point is always the same: fishing is life and life is fishing.

So, I've taken the words of the ancient Babylonians, the catfish noodlers of Mississippi, the high priests of the fly rod, the good ol' boys of jig and pig, the best-known writers on the sport, presidents and poets, and put them here in one place. I've tried to arrange them in something that resembles order. You might think that some of the quotes in a chapter don't really fit, aren't that funny, or you might know a better one. I couldn't include them all, even if I knew them all. And I don't, not by a long shot. The quotes I've chosen just appealed to me on some gut level. I've taken lines from the great writers and their great works, like Izaak Walton and Dame Juliana Berners, in my opinion the first true commentators on the sport of "fyshynge with an angle," the words of Hemingway, Paul Quinnett, Lefty Kreh, and of course from the Internet. I feel lucky to have read in their entirety some of the books listed throughout these pages and doubly lucky to have stumbled across the words of wisdom contained in them all.

My hope is that you will find this book funny and truthful, and that you will see a bit of yourself in the words of others. And I hope you get a belly laugh or at least a good chuckle or two.

Tight lines.

—Damian Rubino
Lyme, Connecticut
December 2006

THE
TRUE
FANATIC

Show me a man who fishes in winter,
and I'll show you a fanatic. Actually, I'll
get the better of the deal, because for
sheer spectacle a fanatic doesn't hold
a candle to a man who fishes in winter.

—PATRICK F. McMANUS
FROM
THEY SHOOT CANOES, DON'T THEY?

I think it's time for me to get out [of fishing], because at the moment I'm only thinking about fishing 21 hours a day, and they're the waking moments.

—REX HUNT
AUSSIE T.V. PERSONALITY,
FOOTBALLER, FISHERMAN

[F]or I love any discourse of rivers, and fish and fishing; the time spent in such discourse passes away very pleasantly.

—IZAAK WALTON
"GRAND-PÈRE" OF FISHING
WRITERS, FROM
THE COMPLEAT ANGLER

[W]hen I was a child starting out, I fished for two and a half years and never even caught a fish, but I kept at it.

—JOHN BAILEY

AUTHOR AND ANGLER, QUOTED IN
THE FISHING CLUB **BY BOB RICH**

I came from a race of fishers; trout streams gurgled about the roots of my family tree.

—JOHN BURROUGHS
AMERICAN NATURE ESSAYIST
AND THE FIRST BIOGRAPHER
OF WALT WHITMAN

Our tradition is that of the first man who sneaked away to the creek when the tribe did not really need fish.

—RODERICK HAIG-BROWN
WRITER, MAGISTRATE, PIONEER
CONSERVATIONIST, FISHERMAN

At the outset, the fact should be recognized that the community of fishermen constitutes a separate class or sub-race among the inhabitants of the earth.

—GROVER CLEVELAND
FISHERMAN AND 22ND PRESIDENT
OF THE UNITED STATES

The angling fever is a very real disease
and can only be cured by the application
of cold water and fresh, untainted air.

—THEODORE GORDON
  INVENTOR OF THE QUILL GORDON,
  ONE OF THE FIRST AMERICAN
  DRY FLIES

All Americans believe that they are born fishermen. For a man to admit a distaste for fishing would be like denouncing mother-love or hating moonlight.

—JOHN STEINBECK
AMERICAN AUTHOR

One of the turning points in my life was when I got my first bait-casting outfit.

—JIMMY CARTER
FISHERMAN AND 38TH PRESIDENT
OF THE UNITED STATES

When this little trout chomped down on the kernel, I pulled the fish out. A huge grin crossed my face, and I was so excited I probably wet myself. But at least I had an excuse. I was still in diapers.

—MIKE IACONELLI
2003 BASSMASTER CHAMPION

To live is not necessary,
to fish is necessary.

—LATIN SAYING

I consider John Goddard to be the finest trout fisherman I have ever fished with, and I have been fortunate to fish with many fabulous—and famous—trout anglers around the world.

—LEFTY KREH
ON JOHN GODDARD,
INTERNATIONAL FISHERMAN,
ENTOMOLOGIST, AUTHOR,
PHOTOGRAPHER, GUIDE,
FROM THE FOREWORD
TO GODDARD'S
A FLY FISHER'S REFLECTIONS

Of course I liked [President Jimmy] Carter. Charlie Fox and Ben Schley taught him a lot about fishing, and he ties a good fly. Reagan couldn't tie his shoes if his life depended on it.

—DICK BLALOCK

FORMER U.S. FOREIGN SERVICE OFFICER, COLLEGE FOOTBALL PLAYER, FISHERMAN, QUOTED IN *FLY FISHING THROUGH THE MIDLIFE CRISIS*, BY HOWELL RAINES

Fishermen don't yield to the weather.

—JACK MacKINNON

If you go fishing often enough, pretty soon the really respectable people will start to avoid you.

—PAUL QUINNETT
NATIONALLY KNOWN
PSYCHOLOGIST, AUTHOR,
FISHING HUMORIST,
FROM *FISHING LESSONS*

From birth to death anyone can fish.

—REX HUNT
AUSSIE T.V. PERSONALITY,
FOOTBALLER, FISHERMAN

[T]o reach my pool, I had to wade across the riffle above the logjam and then work my way around a humongous dead cow inflated to a height of five feet at the ribcage. The smell was overpowering but I needed to get to that pool.

—THOMAS McGUANE
FROM *THE LONGEST SILENCE*

I am, Sir, a brother of the Angle, and therefore an enemy to the Otter.

—IZAAK WALTON
"GRAND-PÈRE" OF FISHING
WRITERS, FROM
THE COMPLEAT ANGLER

[M]arlin fishing is like being on dope. . . .
You catch one that's a hundred pounds,
and then you want to catch one that's
two hundred pounds; then you want to
catch a bigger one and a bigger one
and a bigger one.

—DON TYSON

CHICKEN KING, BLUE WATER
FISHERMAN, QUOTED IN *THE
FISHING CLUB* BY BOB RICH

At the Compleat Angler Hotel, where Hemingway resided much of his time on Bimini, you can see photographs of the writer holding his Tommy gun beside gargantuan dead sharks. Such was his strength and prowess as an angler that he landed the first unmutilated bluefin tuna brought to the Bimini dock.

—FRED WAITZKIN
FROM *THE LAST MARLIN*

To the fisherman born there is nothing so provoking of curiosity as a fishing rod in a case.

—ROLAND PERTWEE
"THE RIVER GOD"

Larry Nixon . . . you could drop [him]
blindfolded onto any body of water
in the world and he'd still catch fish.

—MIKE IACONELLI

**2003 BASSMASTER CHAMPION, ON
ONE OF HIS FELLOW CHAMPIONS**

For twenty years, let us say, a [fishing] purist's life is completely filled by his efforts to convert all reasonable men to his own particular method of taking trout.

—JOHN TAINTOR FOOTE
THE WEDDING GIFT: AND OTHER ANGLING STORIES

I needed a goal, a purpose, a direction in my life, so I set out to fish every mile of blue-ribbon trout water in Montana.

—DAVE AMES
FROM *A GOOD LIFE WASTED*

FISH IN ALL THEIR FORMS

The fish is not so much your quarry
as your partner.

—ARNOLD GINGRICH

FOUNDER OF *ESQUIRE* MAGAZINE,
FISHERMAN

The salmon is accounted the king of fresh-water fish. . . .

—IZAAK WALTON

"GRAND-PÈRE" OF FISHING
WRITERS, FROM
THE COMPLEAT ANGLER

A bass is a bass wherever
it may live.

—JOHN HOPE, FISHING FANATIC

To my purist trout fishing friends, bass are lowly green fish and brown fish. To me, bass are bent rods and aching arms.

—JIM SLINSKY

FOUNDER, PRODUCER, AND HOST OF THE "OUTDOOR TALK NETWORK"

The water makes the fish.

—MEXICAN SAYING

The codfish lays a thousand eggs

The homely hen lays one.

The codfish never cackles

To tell you what she's done.

And so we scorn the codfish

While the humble hen we prize

Which only goes to show you

That it pays to advertise.

—ANONYMOUS AMERICAN RHYME

I know you saltcod, although you come disguised.

—MEXICAN SAYING

Since the armor of a big gar
can flatten a bullet, the talons
of a hawk probably don't feel
like much more than a back rub.

—ROB BUFFLER AND TOM DICKSON
ON WHY THE GAR HAS FEW
PREDATORS, FROM
FISHING FOR BUFFALO

An eel escapes from a good fisherman.

—FRENCH PROVERB

I wondered at the force that drove an eight-ounce [spawning] bluegill to attack a four-pound bass, and I remembered teenage testosterone.

—DAVE AMES
FISHING BUM, GUIDE, AND AUTHOR, FROM *TRUE LOVE AND THE WOOLLY BUGGER*

Different fields, different grasshopper;
different seas, different fish.

—INDONESIAN PROVERB

I'll bet we kin ketch us a cattywampus in one o' them ponds.

—MARJORIE KINNAN RAWLINGS
"JODY'S BASS," FROM
THE YEARLING

You don't catch things like this [a halibut] with a rod. You hunt them with packs of dogs.

—SETH NORMAN
THE FLY FISHER'S GUIDE TO CRIMES OF PASSION

In truth, until a few years ago I more or less despised the sand bass as an alien introduced species fit only for such mechanized pursuit in such artificial waters. But in a live stream on light tackle they subvert that sort of purism, snapping up flies or jigs or live minnows with abandon and battling all the way.

—JOHN GRAVES
"FISHING THE RUN," FROM
A JOHN GRAVES READER

The grass carp [capable of reaching 100 pounds] is actually a member of the minnow family, a gigantic vegetarian one at that, a testament of what can happen to you little fishes if you eat all your spinach.

—SEBASTIAN O'KELLY
ONE OF THE "BROWN WATER
BOYS," FROM
THE OFFBEAT ANGLER

Bonefish are ready takers of a well-presented fly but once hooked, they are so explosive that getting rid of slack line and getting the fish on the reel can produce humiliating results. Their speed and power are so out of proportion to their size that a bonefish, finally landed seems to have gone through a magical reduction from the brute that burned line off against the shrieking drag to the demure little fellow one holds in one's hand while gently removing the fly.

—THOMAS McGUANE
"WEATHER," IN *THE GREATEST FISHING STORIES EVER TOLD*

I want a fish that is fastidious and finicky, wily and skitterish, hard to lure, game when hooked. . . . I am hard to please; but there is, among all the many kinds of fish that swim, one, just one, that fulfills all my many requirements.

—WILLIAM HUMPHREY
MY MOBY DICK

A man set for blue marlin is not interested in catching barracudas. They merely spoil baits. . . .

—PHILIP WYLIE
"LISTEN TO THIS TALE OF WOE,"
FROM *A TREASURY OF TRUE*

My first encounter with a pickerel nearly caused me to give up fishing forever.

—WILLIAM TAPPLY
GONE FISHIN'

This hammerhead [shark] was a projec-
tile. A roostertail of white water flared
from its dorsal as emphatically as it
would from a high-speed outboard.

—JOHN N. COLE
"THE MARQUESAS," FROM
FISHING CAME FIRST

Bluefish do not like summer tourists.
They like people who admire nor'-
easters and don't mind a little rain
and a squall or so.

—ROBERT C. RUARK
IN THE VOICE OF HIS
GRANDFATHER ("THE OLD MAN"),
"SEPTEMBER SONG," FROM
THE OLD MAN AND THE BOY

I yield to no one in love and admiration for the brook trout. I was perfectly familiar with it before I ever saw a black bass; but I am not so blinded by prejudice but that I can share that love with the black bass, which for several reasons is destined to become the favorite game-fish of America.

—JAMES HENSHALL
BOOK OF THE BLACK BASS

Pike—Great Northern. A fish that packs brass knuckles on his jaws and a black-jack in his tail.

—BEN EAST
"BRUISERS OF THE WEED BEDS,"
FROM *OUTDOORS UNLIMITED*

I thought of the waters off Bimini as Hemingway's Garden of Plenty, a gorgeous blue world landscaped with tuna, marlin, broadbill, shark, kingfish, wahoo, cero mackerel, grouper. It was a child's vision of inmutability.

—FRED WAITZKIN
FROM *THE LAST MARLIN*

No fish, neither largemouth nor rainbow nor striper nor salmon, punches as hard as a full-bodied smallmouth.

—W. D. WETHERELL

"SEPTEMBER 18," FROM

ONE MORE RIVER

Mooneye [a.ka. the freshwater tarpon] . . . [w]hen hooked . . . cut back and forth in the current like a crazed sunfish, often flying out of the water.

—ROB BUFFLER AND TOM DICKSON
FISHING FOR BUFFALO

When I opened up a 4½ pound lunker [bass] . . . what did I find? Two field mice each about 5 inches long, two minnows about 4 inches long, and one 5-inch minnow with its tail just showing in the trout's throat. Here was this jasper making like the filling of knockwurst and wants a bucktail, yet!

—JOE BROOKS

"FISHING STREAMERS AND BUCKTAILS," FROM *THE COMPLETE BOOK OF FLY FISHING*

I don't know of any fish that gives as much pleasure to so many fishermen as the ubiquitous striper. He may not be as dazzling as a bonefish or as much a roughneck as a snook, but he covers more ground than these fish do and so comes into contact with more people. Praise the striper . . . the most democratic fish that swims.

—ELLINGTON WHITE
SPORTS ILLUSTRATED WRITER,
FROM "STRIPED BASS AND
SOUTHERN SOLITUDE"
IN *FISHERMAN'S BOUNTY*,
EDITED BY NICK LYONS

The cod's greed makes it easy to catch, but the fish is not much fun for sportsmen.

—MARK KURLANSKY
FROM *COD*

And you may take notice, that as the carp is accounted the water-fox, for his cunning; so the roach is accounted the water-sheep, for his simplicity or foolishness.

—IZAAK WALTON
"GRAND-PÈRE" OF FISHING WRITERS, FROM
THE COMPLEAT ANGLER

Just once I wanted to catch a fish that can eat a man. There is something wonderfully leveling about this arrangement between man and piranha: If we catch them, we eat them; if they catch us, they eat us.

—PAUL QUINNETT
NATIONALLY KNOWN
PSYCHOLOGIST, AUTHOR,
FISHING HUMORIST,
FROM *FISHING LESSONS*

It has been calculated that if no accident prevented the hatching of the eggs and each egg reached maturity, it would take only three years to fill the sea so that you could walk across the Atlantic dryshod on the backs of cod.

—ALEXANDRE DUMAS
  LE GRANDE DICTIONNAIRE
  DE CUISINE

"Tarpon!" I had never been scared of a fish before, but I was now.

—DAVE AMES
FISHING BUM, GUIDE,
AND AUTHOR,
FROM *TRUE LOVE AND
THE WOOLLY BUGGER*

No living thing is more particular about his table manners than a trout. . . .

—ROLAND PERTWEE
FISH ARE SUCH LIARS

Tarpon fishing by night is exciting work, somewhat too exciting for many people.

—J. TURNER, FISHERMAN

The cat-fish is a voracious creature, not at all nice in feeding, but one who, like the vulture, contents himself with carrion when nothing better can be had.

—JOHN JAMES AUDUBON

Carp suck. They slurp down food with a sound suggestive of a drunk walking his lips through a beer puddle on a Formica bar.

—LIONEL ATWILL
SPORTS AFIELD

Anyone who has battled and then released a 6-pound river redhorse while
standing waist deep in a clear northern
Wisconsin wilderness river knows the
joys of roughfishing.

—ROB BUFFLER AND TOM DICKSON
FISHING FOR BUFFALO

Compare the strong bull of Bashan
with a saltwater smelt. Who doubts the
superiority of the bull? Yet, if you drop
them both into the Atlantic ocean, I
will take my chances with the smelt.

—THOMAS BRACKETT REED
**19TH-CENTURY CONGRESSMAN
FROM MAINE**

FISHING AND RELATION-SHIPS

Fishing is such great fun,
I have often felt, that it
really ought to be done
in bed.

—ROBERT TRAVER

**NOM DE PLUME OF JOHN VOELKER,
AUTHOR, MICHIGAN SUPREME
COURT JUSTICE, FISHERMAN**

Fly-fishing is the most fun you can have standing up.

—ARNOLD GINGRICH
FOUNDER OF *ESQUIRE* MAGAZINE,
FISHERMAN

Come live with me, and be my love

And we will some new pleasures prove

Of golden sands, and crystal brooks

With silken lines and silver hooks.

—JOHN DONNE
"THE BAIT"

My wife said I have so many fly rods and reels that I cannot possibly use them all. My reply was that I had rods and reels to fish, rods and reels to tinker with, and then my fine crafted rods and reels to fondle and admire, while dreaming of trout fishing during the cold winter months. You can imagine what kind of look she gave me.

—JIMMY D. MOORE
FLY TIER AND SOUTHERN WIT

The Domestic Tranquility Index (or D.T.I.) is a measure of marital bliss. It is the single most important factor in determining how many fish you will catch over the course of your lifetime, because is determines whether or not you will even be allowed out of the house.

—DAVE AMES

FISHING BUM, GUIDE, AND AUTHOR, FROM *TRUE LOVE AND THE WOOLLY BUGGER*

My biggest worry is that my wife [when I'm dead] will sell my fishing gear for what I said I paid for it.

—KOOS BRANDT, FISHING FANATIC

Bass fishermen watch Monday Night Football, drink beer, drive pickup trucks and prefer noisy women with big breasts. Trout fishermen watch MacNeil-Lehrer, drink white wine, drive foreign cars with passenger-side airbags and hardly think about women at all.

This last characteristic may have something to do with the fact that trout fishermen spend most of the time immersed up to the thighs in ice-cold water.

—*THE NEW YORKER* MAGAZINE

Fly fishing is like sex, everyone thinks there is more than there is, and that everyone is getting more than their share.

—HENRY KANEMOTO
AUTHOR AND FLY TIER

In fact, there are no two things I can think of that go together better than sex and fishing, unless they are fishing and sex.

—PAUL QUINNETT

NATIONALLY KNOWN
PSYCHOLOGIST, AUTHOR,
FISHING HUMORIST,
FROM *FISHING LESSONS*

Hell, if I'd jumped on all the dames I'm supposed to have jumped on, I'd have had no time to go fishing.

—CLARK GABLE
ACTOR

I look quite good in waders. I love my
waders. I don't think there is anything
sexier than just standing in waders
with a fly rod.

—LINDA HAMILTON
ACTRESS

I was bored at one of the parties I was attending, and so pulled [Rudyard] Kipling away from his friends and took him fishing.

—JULIETTE G. LOW, FOUNDER OF THE GIRL SCOUTS

An angler is a man who spends rainy days sitting around on the muddy banks of rivers doing nothing because his wife won't let him do it at home.

—ANONYMOUS

Somebody just back of you while you are fishing is as bad as someone looking over your shoulder while you write a letter to your girl.

—ERNEST HEMINGWAY
AMERICAN AUTHOR AND
TRUE FISHING FANATIC

To my ex-wife, bass are the bewilderment of addiction.

—JIM SLINSKY
FOUNDER, PRODUCER,
AND HOST OF THE
"OUTDOOR TALK NETWORK"

Even a fish wouldn't get into trouble if he kept his mouth shut.

—KOREAN PROVERB

I'd been fishing for more than three times as many years as she [his daughter] had been on earth, but she often caught more than I because she stayed with the job, whereas I have a long-standing tendency to stare at birds in willow trees, or study currents and rocks, or chew platitudes with other anglers randomly encountered.

—JOHN GRAVES
"FISHING THE RUN,"
FROM *A JOHN GRAVES READER*

WANTED: ATTRACTIVE YOUNG WIDOW WITH HOUSE OR TRAILER, PICKUP TRUCK AND BASS BOAT. SEND PICTURES OF BASS BOAT.

—POPULAR BUMPER STICKER

As a boy, I was confused that fishing was a source of tension in our home. I believed that if we kept trolling plentiful waters, Mom and Dad would get along while we made great catches, and our family would prosper and endure; but Mother wasn't interested in dropping a line or even coming on the boat. Dad was the fisherman.

—FRED WAITZKIN
FROM *THE LAST MARLIN*

Finally, though, I went back to [dreaming of] trout fishing, because I found I could remember all the streams and there was always something new about them, while the girls, after I had thought about them a few times, blurred and I could not call them into my mind and finally they all blurred and all became rather the same and I gave up thinking about them almost altogether.

—ERNEST HEMINGWAY

IN THE VOICE OF NICK ADAMS
FROM THE SHORT STORY
"NOW I LAY ME"

I once briefly dated a woman who thought that all trout streams looked alike. The first one I took her to was lovely, the second interesting, the third a pleasant reminder of the first two. The fourth apparently began a redundancy that quickly led to trouble.

—CHRISTOPHER CAMUTO
AUTHOR OF
A FLY FISHERMAN'S BLUE RIDGE

My favorite method of preserving live bait is to store it in the refrigerator until it is ready for use. There are two schools of thought on the proper execution of this procedure. Some hold it is better to tell your wife first and the others claim it is better to let her make the discovery herself.

—PATRICK F. McMANUS

FROM

THEY SHOOT CANOES, DON'T THEY?

Without exception, they [fisherwomen] are tenacious, persevering, and keenly in touch with their native instincts. To them, fishing is a reflective act, a state of mind, and a metaphor for life in how each one views herself in alignment with the universe.

—LYLA FOGGIA
REEL WOMEN

The first place prize was fifty-two thousand dollars, and that night we're talking with all these experienced tournament anglers and they're saying we have good karma, and they're inviting us to fish the next tournament. And we're looking at them and they're in their fifties with no wedding rings on and cute Mexican girls on each arm, and Vicki says, "Karl, you aren't going fishing with those guys. No way."

—KEN LONGAKER AND
KARL BRATVOLD
COMMERCIAL AND TOURNAMENT
FISHERMEN, QUOTED IN *THE FISHING CLUB* BY BOB RICH

When you bait your hook with your heart, the fish always bite!

—JOHN BURROUGHS

AMERICAN NATURE ESSAYIST
AND THE FIRST BIOGRAPHER
OF WALT WHITMAN

A real fisherman never gives up.
I told you I'd make an angler
out of my wife; and so I will. It
has been rather difficult. She
is 'dour' in rising, but she is
beginning to take notice of the
fly now.

—HENRY VAN DYKE
"A FATAL SUCCESS"

The whole purpose of summer fishing, the Old Man said, is not to worry about catching fish, but just to get out of the house and set and think a little. Also, the womenfolk are very bad-tempered in the summer. The less you hang around the premises the less trouble you're apt to get in.

—ROBERT C. RUARK
THE OLD MAN AND THE BOY

There would be a lot less divorce in this country if more husbands and wives fished together.

—PATRICK F. McMANUS

FROM

THEY SHOOT CANOES, DON'T THEY?

And ladies really do love outlaws, for about two weeks to a year. It's a fact of fishing guide history.

—DAVE AMES

A GOOD LIFE WASTED

WHY
WE FISH

Why do people go fishing?
Some say they fish to get fish.
This is obviously false.

—JOHN RANDOLPH

I fish because . . . I suspect that men are going along this way for one last time, and I for one don't want to waste the trip. . . .

—ROBERT TRAVER

**NOM DE PLUME OF JOHN VOELKER,
FROM** *TROUT MADNESS*
FOUND IN *TRAVER ON FISHING*
EDITED BY NICK LYONS

There are two types of fishermen—those who fish for sport and those who fish for fish.

—ANONYMOUS

Perhaps fishing is, for me, only an excuse to be near rivers.

—RODERICK HAIG-BROWN
WRITER, MAGISTRATE, PIONEER
CONSERVATIONIST, FISHERMAN

Once an angler, always a fisherman. If we cannot have the best, we will take the least, and fish for minnows if nothing better is to be had.

—THEODORE GORDON
INVENTOR OF THE QUILL GORDON, ONE OF THE FIRST AMERICAN DRY FLIES

I am having trouble explaining trout fishing to my city friends. They think it either idleness or blood lust, and can't imagine why I spend so much time in its pursuit.

—LEANNE SCHREIBER
"MIDSTREAM," FROM *MIDSTREAM*

There are people in the world who see nothing in the angler's occupation but tedium, laziness, cruelty, and lies. . . . Peace be to all such, and a better way—if they can find it—of spending their leisure time, more human, more humane, more fit for an honest man.

—ODELL SHEPARD
OLD-SCHOOL ANGLER AND WRITER, "THREAD OF THE RIVER," FROM *THY ROD AND THY CREEL*

People ask me why I fish. "I can't help myself," I say. "I had an abnormal childhood."

—PAUL QUINNETT
NATIONALLY KNOWN
PSYCHOLOGIST, AUTHOR,
FISHING HUMORIST,
FROM *FISHING LESSONS*

I liked the wild, beautiful country where trout are often found, the solitude of walking along a river and being drawn more completely into the landscape, and how the sound of a fast-flowing stream could wash away my blues.

—BILL BARICH
CRAZY FOR RIVERS

I don't care how big the fish is. I don't even care if the fish gets free before I land it. I just need to make that perfect cast, and get the strike.

—LEON HALE

**HOUSTON AUTHOR AND
NEWSPAPER COLUMNIST**

. . . I was struck immediately and altogether, the way a sonic boom seems to hit you with a pressure wave from all sides at once, that it wasn't just the promise of the creek that waited before me, or even the rest of the day, but the day after, and the day after that, stretching on into a distance I could scarcely contemplate.

—TED LEESON
"DOWN TO ZERO,"
FROM *THE HABIT OF RIVERS*

Fishing is more than fish; it is the vitalizing lure to outdoor life.

—HERBERT HOOVER
FISHERMAN AND 31ST PRESIDENT
OF THE UNITED STATES

The pleasant'st angling is to see
    the fish

Cut with her golden oars [fins] the
    silver stream,

And greedily devour the treacherous
    bait.

—WILLIAM SHAKESPEARE
    FROM *MUCH ADO ABOUT NOTHING*

Fishing is not an escape from life but often a deeper immersion into it, all of it, the good and the awful, the joyous and the miserable, the comic, the embarrassing, the tragic and the sorrowful.

—HENRY MIDDLETON
RIVERS OF MEMORY

Some of the finest moments I ever had on a fishing trip happened when I didn't have the slightest idea where I was, how I got there, or if I would ever get back to a trail or a dirt road.

—CHARLIE ELLIOT
"ADVENTURES IN SOLITUDE,"
FROM *GONE FISHIN'*

There is certainly something in angling that tends to produce a serenity of the mind.

—WASHINGTON IRVING
19TH-CENTURY AMERICAN AUTHOR, FISHERMAN

Fishing should be the exercise of your skills—and its rewards the places it brings you to.

—NEGLEY FARSON
GOING FISHING

The charm of fishing is that it is the pursuit of what is elusive but attainable, a perpetual series of occasions for hope.

—JOHN BUCHAN
SCOTTISH PUBLISHER
AND POLITICIAN

The wildness and adventure that are in fishing still recommend it to me.

—HENRY DAVID THOREAU
WALDEN

Nothing in this world so enlivens my spirit and emotions as the rivers I know. They are necessities. In their clear, swift or slow, generous or coy waters, I regain my powers; I find again those parts of myself that have been lost in cities.

—NICK LYONS
FROM *BRIGHT RIVERS*

FISHING TECHNIQUE

The best time to go fishing is when you
can get away.

—ROBERT TRAVER
NOM DE PLUME OF JOHN VOELKER,
AUTHOR, MICHIGAN SUPREME
COURT JUSTICE, FISHERMAN

The two best times to fish is when it's rainin' and when it ain't.

—PATRICK F. McMANUS
FISHING HUMORIST

You must lose a fly to catch a trout.

—GEORGE HERBERT

WELSH POET AND FISHERMAN

For trouts are tickled best in muddy water.

—SAMUEL BUTLER
BRITISH AUTHOR

Ted Williams said that Ansil was the only man he knew who had eyes better than his own.

—FRED WAITZKIN
FROM *THE LAST MARLIN*.
SAID OF BIMINI BONEFISH GUIDE
ANSIL SAUNDERS

There's no taking trout in dry breeches.

—MIGUEL DE CERVANTES
FROM *DON QUIXOTE*

A bass doesn't grab a plastic worm; it sucks it in, just like you used to do with a strand of spaghetti when mom wasn't looking. Only faster.

—HOMER CIRCLE
A.K.A. "UNCLE HOMER,"
BASS EXPERT,
FROM *BASS WISDOM*

When I was a young girl salmon fishing with my father . . . I made up charm songs and wordhopes to tempt the fish, to cause them to mean biting my hook. I believed they would do it if I asked them well and patiently with the right hope.

—TESS GALLAGHER
POET

Like they say, you can learn more from a guide in one day than you can in three months fishing alone.

—MARIO LOPEZ
ACTOR AND T.V. HOST

Let your hook always be cast. In the pool where you least expect it, will be fish.

—OVID
ROMAN POET,
A.K.A. PUBLIUS OVIDIUS NASO

Bass and cover is similar to peanut butter and jelly. It's like the chicken and the egg.

—MIKE IACONELLI

2003 BASSMASTER CHAMPION

He catches the best fish who angles with a golden hook.

—LATIN PROVERB

It matters not how many fish are in the sea—if you don't have any bait on your hook.

—ANONYMOUS

I fish better with a lit cigar; some people fish better with talent.

—NICK LYONS

FISHERMAN, EDITOR, AUTHOR

In a great River great fish are found,
but take heede, lest you bee drowned.

—GEORGE HERBERT
WELSH POET AND FISHERMAN

The more the eggs, the worse the hatch,

The more the fish, the worse the catch.

—AARON HILL
ENGLISH DRAMATIST AND WRITER

The fish which has once felt the hook, suspects the crooked metal in every food which offers.

—OVID
ROMAN POET.
A.K.A. PUBLIUS OVIDIUS NASO

[T]he typical gamefish strike has less in common with the carnivorous lunge of a lion attacking a tethered goat than with a Dustbuster assaulting a housefly. If you really want to study the striking moment of gamefish, including those oh-so-prissy trout, get a bug light and a Hoover.

—JAMES BABB
EDITOR OF *GRAY'S SPORTING JOURNAL*, **FROM** *A FLY FISHER'S FOUR SEASONS*

Don't go a-fishing to a famous stream.

—ITALIAN PROVERB

The only "impossible" cast is the one you don't make. Get it?

—MIKE IACONELLI
2003 BASSMASTER CHAMPION,
FROM *FISHING ON THE EDGE*

Even that fish may be caught that
strives the hardest against it.

—DANISH PROVERB

It is not easy to tell one how to cast. The art must be acquired by practice.

—CHARLES ORVIS
FOUNDER OF AMERICA'S OLDEST
MAIL ORDER COMPANY

"Crappies like yellow," everyone's granddad used to say, and all those grandpas were right.

—JOHN GIERACH
"MUSIC OF THE SPHERES," FROM
THE VIEW FROM RAT LAKE

Men call salmon "capricious"; but is not the term a cover for their own ignorance about the habits of the fish and the flies they show them, rather than the truthful representation of facts?

—GEORGE KELSON
INVENTOR OF SALMON FLIES
AND A PRECURSOR TO THE
MODERN DISC DRAG MECHANISM

With few firm exceptions, fishing from boats holds little appeal. It has a certain industrial quality about it, a no-nonsense fixation on the business of catching fish, and I'd much rather drift from place to place, working the promising water on foot, which brings you closer to everything.

—TED LEESON
"DOWN TO ZERO,"
FROM *THE HABIT OF RIVERS*

The art of bottom fishing is that of letting the fish come to the fisherman, instead of vice versa. . . . Bottom fishing, in short, is the Thinking Man's fishing.

—LOUIS D. RUBIN
THE EVEN-TEMPERED ANGLER

The Old Man said it was no use fishing or hunting any time except real early in the morning or late in the afternoon, because even a fish or a jack rabbit had too much sense to bustle around in the heat of the day.

—ROBERT C. RUARK

QUOTING HIS GRANDFATHER ("THE OLD MAN"), "SEPTEMBER SONG," FROM *THE OLD MAN AND THE BOY*

If you can avoid drag, you have at least an outside chance of a fish, no matter what other errors you make.

—DATUS PROPER
WHAT THE TROUT SAID

What a brier patch is to a cottontail, weeds are to Old Longnose [the Great Northern Pike].

—BEN EAST

"BRUISERS OF THE WEEDS,"
FROM *OUTDOORS UNLIMITED*

You cannot bring a hook into a fish's mouth unless there is food on it that pleases him.

—DAME JULIANA BERNERS
THE "GRAND DAME" OF FISHING
WRITERS, FROM "THE TREATYSE
OF FYSSHYNGE WITH AN ANGLE"

Warning—this technique [catfish noodling] should not be attempted by small children as they could be drowned or eaten.

[W]hat distinguishes and unites them [catfish noodlers] to a man are shredded skin, hardened scabs, and even permanent scars spider webbed across their bare forearms. They are the badge of the noodler, the hunter of big, dark fish hidden in the shallow lakes, slow rivers, fetid backwaters and murky oxbows that typify the waters of the Middle South.

—SEBASTIAN O'KELLY
ONE OF THE
"BROWN WATER BOYS,"
FROM *THE OFFBEAT ANGLER*

I only began to see things when I tried to think like a trout.

—LEANNE SCHREIBER

"MIDSTREAM" FROM *MIDSTREAM*

If you want to catch lunker trout, use big streamer flies. When a trout reaches 2 ½ to 3 pounds, he has [sic] done with midges, freshwater shrimp and other small fry. He wants to gulp down something big enough to make his stomach sac press against his sides.

—JOE BROOKS
"FISHING STREAMERS AND BUCKTAILS FOR TROUT," FROM *THE COMPLETE BOOK OF FLY FISHING*

One of the first rules in fishing is that there are few rules in fishing that resourceful trout do not manage to break.

—ROBERT TRAVER
NOM DE PLUME OF JOHN VOELKER,
FROM *TROUT MAGIC*

In truth, fishermen should do as fish do in the summer—lie low. We should give the beaches to the sunbathers and admit that during this idle season, when the great fiber-glass fleet rules the waterways, the thing to do is haul in our lines and run for cover.

—ELLINGTON WHITE
SPORTS ILLUSTRATED WRITER,
FROM "STRIPED BASS AND
SOUTHERN SOLITUDE"
IN *FISHERMAN'S BOUNTY*,
EDITED BY NICK LYONS

Show me a bass fisherman who rarely gets snagged and I'll show you one who doesn't catch many bass.

—HOMER CIRCLE
A.K.A. "UNCLE HOMER,"
BASS EXPERT,
FROM *BASS WISDOM*

A truly expert fly fisherman can match the hatch with the precision of an entomologist, because he knows the Latin name of every streamside insect and its exact artificial counterpart, and there are people who would rather cut off their toe with a hatchet than tie on the wrong fly.

—HOWELL RAINES
NEWSPAPERMAN, AUTHOR,
FISHERMAN, FROM *FISHING
THROUGH THE MIDLIFE CRISIS*

It was a great grin worth a thousand words, a shrug every guide should master, a grin explaining why in the same feeding land some trout will take a nymph, some a pupae, and others only a #23 spent-wing midge tied on a hook hand forged in Kenya just after the sunrise on the winter solstice.

—DAVE AMES
  FISHING BUM, GUIDE, AND AUTHOR,
  FROM *TRUE LOVE AND THE*
  WOOLLY BUGGER

A proper tuck cast is not something you'll see in a life-insurance commercial or a Robert Redford movie. It looks less like the caster is performing aerial ballet than like he's having a seizure.

—JAMES BABB

EDITOR OF *GRAY'S SPORTING JOURNAL,* **FROM** *A FLY FISHER'S FOUR SEASONS*

I never knew anybody catch anything, up the Thames [River in London], except minnows and dead cats. . . .

—JEROME K. JEROME
"STORY-TELLING ON THE THAMES"

Sometimes fish are found in obvious places that are not so obvious.

—SEBASTIAN O'KELLY
ONE OF THE
"BROWN WATER BOYS,"
FROM *THE OFFBEAT ANGLER*

The less the fish, dear Scholar,
the greater the skill in catching
of it.

—LEWIS CARROLL
"A CONFERENCE"

People say they get wind knots, they get 'em on dead-calm days in the fall—this is a bad casting knot.

—LEFTY KREH

FLY CASTING WITH LEFTY KREH

Sir Archie has spoken truth in describing Leithen [the poacher of the story] . . . as an artist. His long, straight delicate casts were art indeed. Like thistledown the fly dropped, like thistledown it floated over the head of the salmon, but like thistledown it was disregarded.

—JOHN BUCHAN
"A GALLANT POACHER"

There is no substitute for fishing sense, and if a man doesn't have it, verily he may cast like an angel and still use his creel largely to transport sandwiches and beer.

—ROBERT TRAVER
NOM DE PLUME OF JOHN VOELKER, FROM *TROUT MADNESS*

To be a good angler one must
be a good predator.

—LEE WULFF
FROM *TROUT ON A FLY*

I have tried expressionist flies, but they work only on expressionist fish, like bass, who will leap for any gaudy bauble when they're in the mood.

—LEANNE SCHREIBER

"MIDSTREAM" FROM *MIDSTREAM*

After my brother and I became good fishermen, we realized that our father was not a great fly caster, but he was accurate and stylish and wore a glove on his casting hand. As he buttoned on his glove in preparation to giving us a lesson, he would say, "It is an art that is performed on a four-count rhythm between ten and two o'clock."

—NORMAN MacLEAN
A RIVER RUNS THROUGH IT

Still fisheth he that catcheth one.

—GEORGE HERBERT
WELSH POET AND FISHERMAN

Clocks are for keeping time, they're not much help in fly castin'.

—LEFTY KREH

FLY CASTING WITH LEFTY KREH

FISH
FOR THE
TABLE

[A] trout that doesn't think two jumps and several runs ahead of the average fisherman is mighty apt to get fried.

—BEATRICE COOK

TILL FISH DO US PART

Either fast or eat trout.

—MEXICAN SAYING

It's no fish ye're buying:
it's men's lives.

—SIR WALTER SCOTT

QUOTING A FISHMONGER'S
RESPONSE TO A CUSTOMER
HAGGLING OVER THE PRICE OF
A HADDOCK IN THE ANTIQUARY

Don't cry "fried fish" before they are caught.

—ITALIAN PROVERB

Smoked carp tastes just as good as smoked salmon when you ain't got no smoked salmon.

—PATRICK F. McMANUS
FISHING HUMORIST

Govern a family as you would cook a small fish—very gently.

—CHINESE PROVERB

If I were a jolly archbishop,

On Fridays I'd eat all the fish up—

Salmon and flounders and smelts;

On other days everything else.

—AMBROSE BIERCE
19TH-CENTURY AMERICAN SATIRIST
AND SOCIAL COMMENTATOR

A fish should swim thrice: in water,
in sauce, and in wine.

—GERMAN PROVERB

Fish, to taste good, must swim three times: in water, in butter, and in wine.

—POLISH PROVERB

Trout should be eaten not later than twenty-four hours after they are caught, else one might better eat damp swamp hay crowned with chain-store mayonnaise.

—ROBERT TRAVER
NOM DE PLUME OF JOHN VOELKER,
FROM *TROUT MADNESS*

A good eating fish must be from the sea.

—SPANISH SAYING

To talk and eat fish requires much care.

—MEXICAN SAYING

Enjoy thy stream, O harmless fish;

And when an angler for his dish,

Through gluttony's vile sin,

Attempts, the wretch to pull thee out,

God give thee strength, O gentle trout,

To pull the rascal in!

—JOHN WOLCOT
18TH-CENTURY BRITISH SATIRIST

But for me there is no mystery in the fact that the fish I buy at the market can never replace the fish that I pulled from the edge of the sea and now lies on the cutting board, ready for broiling.

—LAMAR UNDERWOOD
FROM THE INTRODUCTION TO
THE GREATEST FISHING STORIES EVER TOLD

"Throw him back," Penny called. "We don't need him for eatin'. Leave him to grow up as big as t'other one. Then we'll come back and ketch him."

—MARJORIE KINNAN RAWLINGS
"JODY'S BASS,"
FROM *THE YEARLING*

Life is saltfish.

—HALLDÓR LAXNESS
NOBEL PRIZE–WINNING WRITER
FROM ICELAND

. . . I usually put the sandies [sand bass] back too, but not crappie, whose delicate white flesh my clan prizes above that of all other species for the table and, if there are many, for tucking away in freezer packets against a time of shortage.

—JOHN GRAVES
"FISHING THE RUN," FROM
A JOHN GRAVES READER

I feel real sorry for people who never had a chance at broiled bluefish or mackerel when the fish is so fresh you have to kill him before you clean him. Some say that blues and mackerel are too fat and oily, but there are some people who don't like snails or oysters and think carrots are just dandy.

—ROBERT C. RUARK

"SEPTEMBER SONG," FROM

THE OLD MAN AND THE BOY

Fish taken out of the water and fried on the river bank are many times more delicious than those bought at the market. An oak fire, the smell of pine woods, the soft breeze—all seem to add flavor that cannot be obtained under a roof or within the four walls of a house.

—CHARLIE ELLIOT
"ADVENTURES IN SOLITUDE,"
FROM *GONE FISHIN'*

Supper was always early because of his [father's] fishing.

—ERNEST SCHWIEBERT
"THOUGHTS IN COLTSFOOT TIME,"
FROM *DEATH OF A RIVERKEEPER*

Fish are held together with bones. Without bones they would be invertebrates and therefore no more difficult to catch than clams. When I meet someone who does not eat fish because they are "bony," I must assume they do not understand what holds the world together.

—PAUL QUINNETT
NATIONALLY KNOWN
PSYCHOLOGIST, AUTHOR,
FISHING HUMORIST,
FROM *FISHING LESSONS*

A fresh-caught red snapper has a bloom to its flavor that is encountered in no other fish that I have tasted.

—HOWELL RAINES
    **NEWSPAPERMAN, AUTHOR,
    FISHERMAN, FROM** *FISHING
    THROUGH THE MIDLIFE CRISIS*

Fishiest of all fishy places was the Try Pots, which well deserves it name; for the pots there were always boiling chowders. Chowders for breakfast, and chowder for dinner, and chowder for supper, till you begin to look for fish bones coming through your clothes.

—HERMAN MELVILLE
MOBY DICK

Time so hard you cannot deny
That even saltfish and rice we
can hardly buy.

—1940'S CALYPSO SONG BY
NEVILLE MARCANO ("THE TIGER")

Mr. Leopold Bloom ate with relish the inner organs of beasts and fowls. He liked thick giblet soup, nutty gizzards, a stuffed roast heart, liver slices fried with crustcrumbs, fried hencod's roe.

—JAMES JOYCE
ULYSSES

And it is observable, not only that there are fish, as, namely, the whale, three times as big as the mighty elephant . . . but that the mightiest feasts have been of fish.

—IZAAK WALTON

"GRAND-PÈRE" OF FISHING WRITERS, FROM *THE COMPLEAT ANGLER*

What an idiot is man to believe that abstaining from flesh, and eating fish, which is so much more delicate and delicious, constitutes fasting.

—NAPOLEON I,
NAPOLEON BONAPARTE
**KING OF ITALY, MEDIATOR OF
THE SWISS CONFEDERATION,
PROTECTOR OF THE
CONFEDERATION OF THE RHINE**

There is not a pleasanter summer day's amusement than a merry cruise after the Blue-Fish, no pleasanter close to it than the clam-bake, the chowder, and the broiled Blue-Fish, lubricated with champagne.

—FRANK FORRESTER
IDAHO SENATOR

Overcooking trout is as unpardonable a sin as overeating them.

—JAMES BABB
EDITOR OF *GRAY'S SPORTING JOURNAL*, **FROM** *A FLY FISHER'S FOUR SEASONS*

TO BAIT
OR NOT
TO BAIT

Worms I hate, and never use 'em;

And, kindly friends, ne'er abuse 'em.

—J. P. WHEELDON
ANGLER, NATURALIST, PIGEON
AND RABBIT FANCIER

The fisher who catches a starving fish on a fly and then brags because he did not use bait is not only ignorant, but uncommonly full of crap.

—PAUL QUINNETT

NATIONALLY KNOWN PSYCHOLOGIST, AUTHOR, FISHING HUMORIST, FROM *FISHING LESSONS*

The difference between fly fishers and worm dunkers is the quality of their excuses.

—ANONYMOUS

There is no greater fan of fly fishing than the worm.

—PATRICK F. McMANUS
FISHING HUMORIST

Fly fishermen spend hours tying little clumps of fur and feathers on hooks, trying to make a trout fly that looks like a real fly. But nobody has ever seen a natural insect trying to mate with a Fanwing Ginger Quill.

—ED ZERN

FIELD & STREAM WRITER AND FISHING HUMORIST, *HUNTING AND FISHING FROM A TO ZERN*

In the beginning there were fish in the water, and man and worm on land. It was inevitable that the three should get together.

—HOMER CIRCLE
A.K.A. "UNCLE HOMER,"
BASS EXPERT,
FROM *BASS WISDOM*

The most amazin' thing to me is that you could take somethin' made out of wood, plastic, hair, or rubber and create life and entice another living creature like a bass to think that it's real food and come up and eat.

—BILL DANCE
BASS PRO, QUOTED IN
THE FISHING CLUB **BY BOB RICH**

Is it not an art to deceive a trout with an artificial fly?

—IZAAK WALTON
"GRAND-PÈRE"
OF FISHING WRITERS,
FROM *THE COMPLEAT ANGLER*

It seems a bloodthirsty guy . . . would be a natural-born bait fisherman.

—DAVE AMES

FISHING BUM, GUIDE, AND AUTHOR, FROM *TRUE LOVE AND THE WOOLLY BUGGER*

I briefly abandoned fly fishing for trout with my father and brother in favor of bait fishing for catfish with a gang of river rats who were uncharitably characterized by the parent wing of our fly-fishing sect as lowlifes and no-'counts.

—JAMES BABB
EDITOR OF *GRAY'S SPORTING JOURNAL*, FROM *A FLY FISHER'S FOUR SEASONS*

A trout killed with a fly is a jewel of price, but a trout poached with a worm is like throwing cogged dice.

—J. P. WHEELDON
ANGLER, NATURALIST, PIGEON
AND RABBIT FANCIER

Surprisingly, many anglers are ashamed to admit they fish with live bait. . . . Live bait was totally unknown to early cavemen, who had to make do with a rather limited assortment of dry flies, nymphs, and a few streamers.

—PATRICK F. McMANUS
FROM *THEY SHOOT CANOES, DON'T THEY?*

There is much to said, in a world like ours, for taking the world as you find it and for fishing with a worm.

—BLISS PERRY

"FISHING WITH A WORM"

What, you say, chum and fly fish? Isn't that like wearing sneakers and cut-offs to hear the National Symphony play at the Kennedy Center?

—SEBASTIAN O'KELLY
ONE OF THE
'BROWN WATER BOYS,'
FROM *THE OFFBEAT ANGLER*

LIARS AND BRAGGARTS

[O]f all the liars among mankind, the fisherman is the most trustworthy.

—WILLIAM SHERWOOD FOX

SILKEN LINES AND SILVER HOOKS

Nothing makes a fish bigger
than almost being caught.

—ANONYMOUS

Fishermen are born honest,
but they get over it.

—ED ZERN
FIELD & STREAM WRITER
AND FISHING HUMORIST

Some of the biggest fish in Texas are caught by the tale.

—ANONYMOUS

All fishermen are liars; it's an occupational disease with them like housemaid's knee or editor's ulcers.

—BEATRICE COOK
TILL FISH DO US PART

All fishermen are liars except you and me and to tell you the truth, I'm not so sure about you!

—ANONYMOUS

In Texas, the fish seem to grow the most between the moment they strike a lure and the instant they spit it out.

—WALLACE O. CHARITON
TEXAS HUMORIST

Bragging may not bring happiness, but no man having caught a large fish goes home through an alley.

—ANONYMOUS

Even eminent chartered accountants are known, in their capacity as fishermen, blissfully to ignore differences between seven and ten inches, half pound and two pounds, three fish and a dozen fish.

—WILLIAM SHERWOOD FOX
SILKEN LINES AND SILVER HOOKS

For angling-rod he took a sturdy oake;

For line, a cable that in storm ne'er broke;

His hooke was such as heads the end of pole

To pluck down house ere fire consumes it whole;

The hook was baited with a dragon's tail,—

And then on rock he stood to bob for whale.

—SIR WILLIAM DAVENANT
17TH-CENTURY ENGLISH
DRAMATIST

Fishing is a delusion entirely surrounded by liars in old clothes.

—DON MARQUIS
NEW YORK COLUMNIST AND
SHORT STORY WRITER

When Texans start talkin' huntin' or fishin', strap on your waders, 'cause it's gonna get deep in a hurry.

—JIM GRAMON
TEXAS STORYTELLER AND AUTHOR

Anglers . . . exaggerate grossly and make gentle and inoffensive creatures sound like wounded buffalo and man-eating tigers.

—RODERICK HAIG-BROWN
WRITER, MAGISTRATE, PIONEER
CONSERVATIONIST, FISHERMAN

Since my first days on the water, I have been a lucky fish spotter; I have become accustomed to having others doubt my reports simply because they have not seen what my eyes recorded.

—JOHN N. COLE
"THE MARQUESAS,"
FROM *FISHING CAME FIRST*

Every little fish expects
to become a big whale.

—DANISH PROVERB

I could not help but remember the giant marlin Captain had lost in 1928, which we estimated at twenty-two or twenty-three feet, or the twenty-foot one I had raised in Tautira or the twenty-eight foot one the natives had seen repeatedly alongside their canoes.

—ZANE GREY
"THE FIRST THOUSAND POUNDER,"
FROM *ZANE GREY: OUTDOORSMAN*

We ask a simple question

And that is all we wish:

Are fishermen all liars?

Or do only liars fish?

—WILLIAM SHERWOOD FOX

SILKEN LINES AND SILVER HOOKS

From that pool [on the Yellowstone River] I've taken enough big trout . . . that if they were laid end to end they would reach from Denver to the Rio Grande.

—JOE BROOKS
*THE COMPLETE BOOK
OF FLY FISHING*

And the mighty sturgeon, Nahma,

Said to Ugudwash, the sun-fish,

To the bream, with scales of crimson,

"Take the bait of this great boaster,

Break the line of Hiawatha!"

—HENRY WADSWORTH LONGFELLOW,
THE SONG OF HIAWATHA

When a fisherman is going to tell you about the big musky he caught, he knows you will subtract ten pounds to allow for his untruthfulness.

So he adds ten pounds to allow for your subtraction.

The other ten pounds he adds on account of being such a liar.

—ED ZERN

FIELD & STREAM **WRITER AND FISHING HUMORIST,** *HUNTING AND FISHING FROM A TO ZERN*

I have made it a matter of policy to disbelieve all fishing stories on their first telling; they begin to have the ring of truth, however, after I've repeated them several times.

—PAUL QUINNETT
NATIONALLY KNOWN
PSYCHOLOGIST, AUTHOR,
FISHING HUMORIST,
FROM *FISHING LESSONS*

The poor groundlings who can find no better use for a river than something to put a bridge over think all fishermen are liars.

—ROLAND PERTWEE
"THE RIVER GOD"

Give me the patience to sit calmly by,

While amateurs with veterans gravely vie,

Recounting deeds with rod and fly,

Then help me tell the FINAL, CROWNING LIE!

—C. J. JUDD

It must, of course, be admitted that large stories of fishing adventure are sometimes told by fishermen—and why should this not be so? Beyond all question there is no sphere of human activity so full of strange and wonderful incidents as theirs.

—GROVER CLEVELAND
22ND AND 24TH PRESIDENT OF THE UNITED STATES

Some people are under the impression that all that is required to make a good fisherman is the ability to tell lies easily and without blushing. . . .

—JEROME K. JEROME
"STORY-TELLING ON THE THAMES

I never lost a little fish—yes,

I am free to say

It always was the biggest fish I caught

That got away.

—EUGENE FIELD

CHILDREN'S POET

In Florida men sometimes hook and land, on rod and tackle a little finer than a steam-crane and chain, a mackerel-like fish called "tarpon," which sometime run to 120 pounds. Those men stuff their captures and exhibit them in glass cases and become puffed up.

—RUDYARD KIPLING
"ON DRY-COW FISHING
AS A FINE ART"

Trout fishermen [are] regarded in many quarters as tricky and deceitful, subtle and full of guile, and as men who lie just to keep their hands in. But don't blame fishermen: after all they devote their lives to practicing these black arts on the stream, a topsy-turvy world where these vices are hailed as virtues.

—ROBERT TRAVER

NOM DE PLUME OF JOHN VOELKER, FROM *TROUT MADNESS*

I envy not him that eats better meat than I do, nor him that is richer, or that wears better clothes than I do; I envy nobody but him, and him only that catches more fish than I do.

—IZAAK WALTON
"GRAND-PÈRE" OF ALL FISHING WRITERS, *THE COMPLEAT ANGLER*

VARIATIONS ON A THEME

THE ORIGINAL . . .

Give a man a fish, and you feed him for
a day. Teach a man to fish, and you
feed him for a lifetime.

—LAO TZU
CHINESE PROVERB

VARIATIONS . . .

Give a man a fish, and you feed him for a day.
Teach a man to fish, and you feed him for a
lifetime. Unless he doesn't like sushi—then you
have to teach him to cook.

> —AUREN HOFFMAN, AMERICAN
> INTERNET ENTREPENEUR

Give a man a fish, and you feed him for a day.
Teach a man to fish, and you feed him for a lifetime. Teach a man to sell fish and he eats steak.

> —ANONYMOUS

Give a man a fish, and he has food for a day;
teach him how to fish, and you can get rid of
him for the entire weekend.

> —ZENNA SCHAFFER
> AUTHOR

GIVE A MAN A FISH, AND YOU FEED HIM FOR A DAY. TEACH A MAN TO FISH, AND . . .

you will not have to listen to his incessant whining about how hungry he is.

—ANONYMOUS

you can sell him fishing equipment.

—ANONYMOUS

he will sit in a boat and drink beer all day.

—ANONYMOUS

he'll be dead of mercury poisoning inside of three years.

—CHARLES HAAS
PROFESSOR OF
ENVIRONMENTAL ENGINEERING

he'll write a book about fishing.

—DAMIAN RUBINO

VARIATIONS ON THE VARIATION . . .

Give a man a fish, and you'll feed him for a day;
give him a religion, and he'll starve to death while
praying for a fish.

—ANONYMOUS

Teach a man to fish, and you introduce another
competitor into the overcrowded fishing industry.
Give a man a fish, and you stimulate demand for
your product.

—ANONYMOUS

Give a man a fish, and you leave yourself wide open to lawsuits. Teach a man to fish, and he'll ask for an ocean.

—ANONYMOUS

Give a woman a fish, and you'll be sleeping on the couch again.

—ANONYMOUS

Give a man a fish, and he'll wonder what you want from him.

—ANONYMOUS

SAVE
OUR
FISHES!

Who hears the fishes
when they cry?

—HENRY DAVID THOREAU

I used to be shocked by at the condition of most roach or dace I caught in rivers that were popular match [fishing tournament] venues. Mouths that were ripped and cut, others raw with fungus growing and some with missing lips that had been ripped off by the match fisherman in his haste to remove the hook.

—JOHN GODDARD
INTERNATIONAL FISHERMAN,
ENTOMOLOGIST, AUTHOR,
PHOTOGRAPHER, GUIDE. FROM
A FLY FISHER'S REFLECTIONS

Well, I love fishing. I wouldn't kill a fly myself but I've no hesitation in killing a fish. A lot of men are like that. No bother. Out you come. Thump. And that's not the only reason.

—NORMAN MacCAIG

20TH-CENTURY SCOTTISH POET

[T]he waters are Nature's store-house, in which she locks up her wonders.

—IZAAK WALTON
"GRAND-PÈRE"
OF FISHING WRITERS,
FROM *THE COMPLEAT ANGLER*

And although all the rivers [of the Blue Ridge Mountains] eventually run unto the sea, most detour now through mall fountains from Fairfax to Spartanburg, jetting ignominiously for a few seconds into the greenish glow that keeps shoppers schooled at store counters like bream at the edge of a pond.

—CHRISTOPHER CAMUTO
AUTHOR, FROM
A FLY FISHERMAN'S BLUE RIDGE

All drains lead to the ocean.

—GILL
FROM *FINDING NEMO*

Little streams make big rivers.

—SPANISH SAYING

Catch and Release fishing is a lot like golf. You don't have to eat the ball to have a good time.

—ANONYMOUS

Game fish are too valuable to be caught only once.

—LEE WULFF
THE GODFATHER OF
CATCH AND RELEASE

The great privilege is the moment one is released, when the small, strong fish moves from your hand to renew its hold upstream. Then it's time to go.

—THOMAS McGUANE
FROM *THE LONGEST SILENCE*

The fish bounded at his [the fisherman's] touch, and lay still again. He saw its strong shoulders, the saffron of its fins and the splendid play of colours over it whole glowing body, and he could not find it in his heart to kill the fish.

—PATRICK O'BRIAN
"THE RETURN,"
FROM *THE RENDEZVOUS*

I gave the fish back to the river, or gave it back to them: shapely, forktailed, bright-silver creatures with thin dark parallel striping along their sides, gaping rhythmically from the struggle's exhaustion as they eased away backward from my hand in the slow shallows.

—JOHN GRAVES
"FISHING THE RUN,"
FROM *A JOHN GRAVES READER*

This is my kind of fishin'.
It ain't murder—it's *fishin'*.

—ROBERT C. RUARK

**IN THE VOICE OF HIS
GRANDFATHER ("THE OLD MAN"),
"SEPTEMBER SONG" FROM**
THE OLD MAN AND THE BOY

This could be the beginning of the end of Lake Erie's fabulous walleye fishing.

—DAVE KELCH
OHIO STATE UNIVERSITY
SEA GRANT PROGRAM,
COMMENTING ON THE INVASION
OF THE ZEBRA MUSSEL,
FROM *FISHING FOR BUFFALO*

I will never kill another trout. I release every one I catch, no matter what the regulations call for. There are too few of them in the world, and each one is too precious to do something as wasteful as eating it.

—DICK BLALOCK

LEGENDARY MARYLAND FISHING GUIDE, IN *FISHING THROUGH THE MIDLIFE CRISIS*, **BY HOWELL RAINES**

Perhaps nothing compares in angling to seeing a thousand-pound fish leap fifteen feet in the air, shaking its head violently to dislodge the hook as its ten-foot body cartwheels in the air to crash against the water. Nothing in angling is as physically challenging as bringing such a fish to the gaff. And nothing in angling takes as much moral courage as releasing that extraordinary predator to live and fight again.

—HERBERT A. SCHAFFNER
SALTWATER GAME FISH IN NORTH AMERICA

The herring are not in the tides
as they

Were of old;

My sorrow for many a creak gave
the creel

In the cart

That carried the take to Sligo Town
to be sold . . .

—WILLIAM BUTLER YEATS
"THE MEDITATION OF
THE OLD FISHERMAN"

The problem with the people in Petty Harbour [Newfoundland] . . . is that they are at the wrong end of a 1,000 year fishing spree.

—MARK KURLANSKY

ON THE DISAPPEARANCE OF THE ATLANTIC COD, FROM *COD*

[Y]es, even politically correct catch-and-release kills fish if done incautiously, and in heavily fished streams with lots of hold-it-higher-toward-the-camera Kodak moments it kills a *lot* of fish. . . .

—JAMES BABB
EDITOR OF *GRAY'S SPORTING JOURNAL*, FROM *A FLY FISHER'S FOUR SEASONS*

If I were to write an account of half the poaching stories that are common to all Salmon rivers, I should produce a book, the dimensions of which would terrify the public, even in this pen-compelling age.

—WILLIAM SCROPE

"THE RIVER SNEAK"

The artificial breeding of domestic fish . . . is apparently destined to occupy an extremely conspicuous place in the history of man's efforts to compensate his prodigal waste of the gifts of nature.

—GEORGE PERKINS MARSH
**FATHER OF THE
ENVIRONMENTAL MOVEMENT**

You must not be too greedy in catching your said game [fish], as in taking too much at one time. . . . That could easily be the occasion of destroying your own sport and other men's also.

—DAME JULIANA BERNERS

"GRAND DAME" OF FISHING
WRITERS, FROM "THE TREATYSE
OF FYSSHYNGE WITH AN ANGLE"

From the Royal Family on down, the gentry are still avid killers of Britain's dwindling supply of the salmonid family, which includes the majority of our cold water game fish.

—HOWELL RAINES
NEWSPAPERMAN, AUTHOR,
FISHERMAN, FROM *FISHING THROUGH THE MIDLIFE CRISIS*

I would no more kill this fish for a picture, or to fill a freezer, than fell a 300-year-old Sequoia for kindling, or swat a hummingbird just to see it hold still.

—SETH NORMAN
THE FLY FISHER'S GUIDE
TO CRIMES OF PASSION

Any society that must specifically outlaw baitfishing in a catch-and-release trout stream acknowledges that its citizens will do anything that isn't specifically forbidden, while the rest of society turns a blind eye.

—WILLIAM TAPPLY
GONE FISHIN'

Fishing tournaments
seem a little like playing
tennis with living balls. . . .

—JIM HARRISON

JUST BEFORE DARK

A rodless Walton of the brooks,

A bloodless sportsman I.

—SAM WALTER FOSS
THE BLOODLESS SPORTSMAN

Catching trout is a sport. Eating them is not.

—LEE WULFF

FROM *TROUT ON A FLY*

.

ODES TO A BEAUTIFUL SPORT

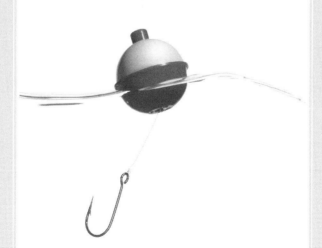

Who but an angler knows that magic hour when the red lamp of summer drops behind blackening hemlocks and the mayflies emerge from the folds of their nymphal robes to dance in a ritual as old as the river itself?

—A. J. McCLANE
"SONG OF THE ANGLER,"
FROM *THE COMPLEAT McCLANE*

Give me autumn, I say, with the black-flies and tourists all gone with the wind, and the leaves just tingeing crimson and gold, and the trout trading their spring-time paranoia for bacchanalian autumnal feasting, bulking up like everyone and everything in New England for the long gestational winter.

—JAMES BABB
EDITOR OF *GRAY'S SPORTING JOURNAL*, FROM *A FLY FISHER'S FOUR SEASONS*

Soon the pond will move into its evening program. The bass and the larger panfish will come out of the deep water to nose into the shallows. This they'll do to the music of the spheres—the turning of the planet that drops the sun, slants the light, cools the water, and brings the fish to the surface.

—JOHN GIERACH
"MUSIC OF THE SPHERES,"
FROM *THE VIEW FROM RAT LAKE*

In a bowl to sea went wise men three,

On a brilliant night in June:

They carry a net, and their hearts were set

On fishing up the moon.

—THOMAS LOVE PEACOCK
"THE WISE MEN OF GOTHAM"

[H]ere at the Marquesas, their wonderful prehistoric, deep-sided, armor-scaled massive shapes glide like shimmering projectiles across the white sand of the channel mouth in water so stunningly clear I have, I swear, seen my reflection in a tarpon's dark globe of an eye as the fish soared under our bow.

—JOHN N. COLE

"THE MARQUESAS,"
FROM *FISHING CAME FIRST*

Though I eventually moved West for much different reasons, I have come to appreciate this one above all others: It rescued me from seasons. They exist here, to be sure, but less a matter of calendars than of inclination and opportunity. Salmon, winter steelhead, whitefish, trout, shad, spring Chinook, trout, smallmouth, simmer steelhead, sea-run cutthroat, salmon—they overlap like the scales of fish, layered three and four deep on some rivers, the smooth skin of a year that is proof against a good many things.

—TED LEESON
"DOWN TO ZERO,"
FROM *THE HABITS OF RIVERS*

I yearned to become part of that world, to be with those fish, those great olive-backed tench as they sauntered down the avenues amidst the weeds across floors of polished sand, into their dark-ened rooms beneath the drapes of lilies.

—JOHN BAILEY
FROM *TROUT AT TEN THOUSAND FEET*

Oh, but that was a scary, desolate beach, the offset currents cutting great sloughs where the big fish lay. The silver-sandy beach came down from the steep dunes as high as mountains, with just a fringe of sea oats.

—ROBERT C. RUARK

"SEPTEMBER SONG," FROM

THE OLD MAN AND THE BOY

I quit fishing entirely, content to lay aside my tackle. Stretching myself prone on the bank with my eyes not more than one foot from the water, I beguiled the time by watching a small trout nearby feeding in the manner of his brother.

—VINCENT C. MARINARO
A MODERN DRY-FLY CODE

I've known the Okefenokee [waters] for a long, long time. . . . One moment it lies in wait like a coiled moccasin. The next it strikes sudden fury that rips open the prairies and whip-lashes the timber in wind and rain. But it is never more terrible than when it sprawls sinister and brooding by its very silence building tension and suspense.

—CHARLIE ELLIOT
"ADVENTURES IN SOLITUDE,"
FROM *GONE FISHIN'*

One great thing about fly fishing is that
after a while nothing exists of the world
except thoughts about fly fishing

—NORMAN MacLEAN
FROM *A RIVER RUN'S THROUGH IT*

And with a cold rain misting through the skeletal black-trunked trees behind the house, such thoughts of fishing, and the butter-colored coltsfoot in the sheltered places, help to pass this wintry season of discontent.

—ERNEST SCHWIEBERT
"THOUGHTS IN COLTSFOOT TIME,"
FROM *DEATH OF A RIVERKEEPER*

A good stretch of river is never the shortest distance between two points. River time is slow and convoluted, and when I concentrate and fish deliberately hours disappear into pools, diffuse themselves in riffles, and contract in the eddies where I wait for good trout to show themselves.

—CHRISTOPHER CAMUTO
AUTHOR OF
A FLY FISHERMAN'S BLUE RIDGE

Rivers.

Bright green live rivers.

The coil and swoop of them, their bright dancing riffles and their flat dimpled pools at dusk.

—NICK LYONS
FROM *BRIGHT RIVERS*

I drifted so far away from Stuart Fork that when a fish hit my lure, it had the effect of yanking me out of the clouds and back into my body. High up leaped a silvery little rainbow, as hooked in the moment as I was.

—BILL BARICH
CRAZY FOR RIVERS

When I'm fishing well, my concentration is so intensely focused on the surface of the stream that I enter a kind of trance, from which I emerge startled by some sudden sound or change in light. I'll look up, as if just awakened from a dream, and see a great blue heron taking flight at my approach. . . .

—LEANNE SCHREIBER
"MIDSTREAM," FROM *MIDSTREAM*

Time is but the stream I go a-fishing in

I drink at it; but while I drink I see the sandy bottom and

detect how shallow it is. Its thin current slides away, but

eternity remains. I would drink deeper; fish in the sky,

where the bottom is pebbly with stars.

—HENRY DAVID THOREAU
WALDEN

This time it took three casts and then again I almost jumped out of my waders when a hook-beaked beezer poked his nose out and clapped his mandibles at me.

—JOE BROOKS
"FISHING STREAMERS AND BUCKTAILS FOR TROUT,"
FROM *THE COMPLETE BOOK OF FLY FISHING*

And angling too, that solitary vice,

What Izaak Walton sings or says:

The quaint, old, cruel, coxcomb,
in his gullet

Should have a hook, and a small
trout to pull it.

—LORD BYRON
DON JUAN

All living waters whisper to us.

—HOWELL RAINES
NEWSPAPERMAN, AUTHOR,
FISHERMAN, FROM
*FISHING THROUGH
THE MIDLIFE CRISIS*

The white line melted, smoked, burned off the reel.

—ZANE GREY

"THE FIRST THOUSAND-POUNDER,"
FROM *ZANE GREY: OUTDOORSMAN*

Give me mine angle; we'll off to the river: there—

My music playing far off—I will betray

Tawny-finn'd fishes; my bended hook shall pierce

Their slimy jaws; and, as I draw them up,

I'll think them every one an Antony,

And say, "Ah, ha!" you're caught.

—WILLIAM SHAKESPEARE
FROM *ANTONY AND CLEOPATRA*

To his [the fisherman's] eyes the stream brings glitter, ever-changing hues, curves of inimitable and never-failing grace, and the magical effect of motion in the midst of a stable landscape— the leaping white jet of life.

—ODELL SHEPARD
OLD-SCHOOL ANGLER AND
WRITER, FROM
THY ROD AND THY CREEL

Trout are like dreams hovering in the elusive unconscious. In capturing one, if ever so briefly, before release, there is that sense of revelation occurring when one awakens in the night, snatching a dream from the dark portals of sleep.

—KITTY PEARSON-VINCENT
PHOTOGRAPHER, QUOTED IN
FISHING THROUGH THE MIDLIFE CRISIS BY HOWELL RAINES

I immersed myself in the watery world
of fish and fishing: drinking in mystery
and magic, sensing that the objects
of my desires were infinitely noble,
constantly intriguing, eternally amaz-
ing and always beautiful.

—JOHN BAILEY
FROM *TALES FROM THE RIVERBANK*

It is this sort of possession you look for when angling. To watch the river flowing, the insects landing and hatching, the places where trout hold, and to insinuate the supple, binding move-ment of tapered line until, when the combination is right, the line becomes rigid and many of its motions are conceived at the other end.

—THOMAS McGUANE
FROM *THE LONGEST SILENCE*

Exultation is the going

Of an inland soul to sea—

Past the houses, past the headlands

Into deep Eternity!

Bred as we, among the mountains,

Can the sailor understand

The divine intoxication

Of the first league out from land?

—EMILY DICKINSON
"SETTING SAIL,"
FROM *COMPLETE POEMS*

[F]or I wonder has any fisherman ever found that lost fly. The reeds, the buttercups, and the little people with many legs who run in the wet grass conspire together to keep the secret of its hiding place.

—ROLAND PERTWEE
"THE RIVER GOD"

I have heard them all—the youthful voice of the little Beaverkill, the growling of the Colorado as it leaps from its den, the kettledrum pounding of the Rogue, the hiss of the Yellowstone's riffles, the sad sound of the Orinoco, as mournful as a G chord held on a guitar.

—A. J. McCLANE
"SONG OF THE ANGLER,"
FROM *THE COMPLEAT McCLANE*

FISHING
AS
RELIGION

Everyone ought to believe in something. I believe I'll go fishing.

—ANONYMOUS

Fishermen who miss church on holy days are not necessarily out of communication with God.

—PAUL QUINNETT
NATIONALLY KNOWN
PSYCHOLOGIST, AUTHOR,
FISHING HUMORIST,
FROM *FISHING LESSONS*

The gods do not deduct from man's
allotted span the hours spent in fishing.

—BABYLONIAN PROVERB

Some go to church and think about fishing, others go fishing and think about God.

—TONY BLAKE, FISHERMAN

The trout do not rise in the cemetery, so you better do your fishing while you are still able to.

—SPARSE GREY HACKLE
    NOM DE PLUME OF
    ALFRED W. MILLER,
    WRITER FOR *SPORTS ILLUSTRATED*
    AND *OUTDOOR LIFE*

Mortality being what it is, any new river could be your last.

—THOMAS McGUANE
FROM *THE LONGEST SILENCE*

Fishing provides that connection with the whole living world. It gives you the opportunity of being totally immersed, turning back into yourself in a good way. A form of meditation, some form of communion with levels of yourself that are deeper than the ordinary self.

—TED HUGHES
POET

Three-fourths of the Earth's surface is water, and one-fourth is land. It is quite clear that the good Lord intended us to spend triple the amount of time fishing as taking care of the lawn.

—CHUCK CLARK, FISHING FANATIC

Shall I go to heaven or a-fishing?

—HENRY DAVID THOREAU
AMERICAN AUTHOR, NATURALIST,
TAX RESISTER, FISHERMAN

There are only two occasions when Americans respect privacy, especially in Presidents. Those are prayer and fishing.

—HERBERT HOOVER
31ST PRESIDENT OF
THE UNITED STATES

Like many Southerners, I was ruined for church by early exposure to preachers. So when I need to hear the sigh of the Eternal, I find myself drawn to a deep hollow between Fork Mountain Double Top Mountain and the eastern flank of the Blue Ridge [where flows the Rapidan River].

—HOWELL RAINES
NEWSPAPERMAN, AUTHOR,
FISHERMAN, FROM *FISHING
THROUGH THE MIDLIFE CRISIS*

Sitting still and wishing made no person great. The good Lord sends the fishing, but you must dig the bait.

—ANONYMOUS

They that go down to the sea in ships, that do business in great waters; These see the works of the Lord, and his wonders in the deep.

—PSALMS, 107: 23–25

As everyone knows,
meditation and water
are wedded forever.

—HERMAN MELVILLE
MOBY-DICK

Simon Peter said, "I go a-fishing": and they said, "We also go with thee."

—JOHN, 21:3

I don't believe in a literal interpretation of the Bible because somebody had to write the book and it's too good a story and somebody stretched the facts which isn't surprising since it's really a fishing story.

—DAVE AMES

FISHING BUM, GUIDE, AND AUTHOR, FROM *TRUE LOVE AND THE WOOLLY BUGGER*

Not many anglers are
heaven-born.

—R. D. BLACKMORE
"CROCKER'S HOLE"

Lyin' is lyin' be it about fish or money, and is forbid by Scripter. . . . Billy Matison's [one of Butler's characters] got to give up fish-lyin', or he won't never get into the kingdom.

—ELLIS PARKER BUTLER
AMERICAN HUMORIST

"Then you mean that I have got to go on catching these damned two-and-a-half-pounders at this corner forever and ever?"

The keeper nodded.

"Hell!" said Mr. Castwell.

"Yes," said his keeper.

—G. E. M. SKUES
"MR. THEODORE CASTWELL"

If I was a deacon, I wouldn't let a fish's tail whisk the whole Catechism out of my head.

—HENRY WARD BEECHER
CONNECTICUT-BORN
PRESBYTERIAN MINISTER

To the flyfisherman, the hawthorn is an insect. To the trout on the shallows below the Red Gate, it's manna from heaven.

—NEIL PATTERSON

"ROLL CAST," FROM

CHALKSTREAM CHRONICLE

[Trout fishing] is a separate little world, cunningly contrived, with certain codes and rules and icons. It is not a religion, though some believers make it such, and it is less than an art.

—NICK LYONS
FROM *BRIGHT RIVERS*

When a man picks up a fly rod for the first time, he may not know it, he has been born again.

—JOSEPH D. FARRIS, **ANGLER**

If fishing is like religion, then fly fishing is high church.

—TOM BROKAW
NBC NEWS ANCHORMAN

Ye monsters of the bubbling deep,

Your Maker's praises spout;

Up from the sands ye codlings peep,

And wag your tails about.

—COTTON MATHER
PURITAN MINISTER,
SALEM WITCH HUNTER, HYMN

The fishing gods giveth and they taketh away. Amen.

—WILLIAM TAPPLY
GONE FISHIN'

FISHING
VERSUS
WORK

The worst day of fishing is still better than the best day at work.

—DAVE STEMPKO,
WELL-KNOWN FLY TIER

Whoever said, "A bad day of fishing is always better than a good day at work" never had their boat sink.

—ANONYMOUS

[T]his planet is covered with sordid men who demand that he who spends time fishing shall show returns in fish.

—LEONIDAS HUBBARD, JR.
AMERICAN OUTDOOR WRITER

Fishing, with me, has always been an excuse to drink in the daytime.

—JIMMY CANNON

NEW YORK SPORTSWRITER

When you have stopped work to go fishing and then been weathered out, your sense of idleness has no bounds.

—THOMAS McGUANE
FROM *THE LONGEST SILENCE*

[H]anging around the Reagan crowd made me yearn for connection with something noble and uplifting. I bought a fly rod.

—HOWELL RAINES
NEWSPAPERMAN, AUTHOR, FISHERMAN, AFTER HAVING WORKED A NUMBER OF YEARS AS A CORRESPONDENT AT THE WHITE HOUSE, FROM *FISHING THROUGH THE MIDLIFE CRISIS*

[D]on't wait until you retire to go fishing. Don't even wait until your annual vacation. Go at every opportunity. Things that appear more urgent at the moment may, in the long run, turn out to be far less so.

—TED TRUEBLOOD
FIELD & STREAM

Don't talk to me of work!

I'm jest goin' fishin'

Where the speckled beauties lurk,

'Round the pools a-swishin'

Ne'er a thought have I of care,

Settin' on a green bank there,

Drinkin' in the soft June air,

Void of all ambition!

—JOHN KENDRICK BANGS
AMERICAN AUTHOR AND SATIRIST

A certain quality of youth is indispensable to the successful angler, a certain unworldliness and readiness to invest yourself in an enterprise that doesn't pay in the current coin.

—JOHN BURROUGHS
AMERICAN NATURE ESSAYIST
AND THE FIRST BIOGRAPHER
OF WALT WHITMAN

Fish, drink, and be merry—for tomorrow we must cut the grass.

—ROBERT TRAVER
NOM DE PLUME OF JOHN VOELKER,
FROM *TROUT MADNESS*

I only make movies to finance my fishing.

—LEE MARVIN

ACTOR

The truth is that fishing for trout is as crazy and self-indulgent as inhaling opium. What, then, can be said for trout fishing? Simply this: it's got work beat a mile and is, if a man can stand it, indecently great fun.

—ROBERT TRAVER

NOM DE PLUME OF JOHN VOELKER, FROM *ANATOMY OF A FISHERMAN*

The only thing bad about winning the pennant is that you have to manage the All-Star Game the next year. I'd rather go fishing for three years.

—WHITEY HERZOG
BASEBALL COACH

Good fishing days vanish as if they never happened, as if the hours won't be counted against the sum of your life. It's that relative-time thing again, the diametric opposite of a boring job.

—DAVE AMES
A GOOD LIFE WASTED

FISHING
WIT

If people concentrated on the really important things in life, there'd be a shortage of fishing poles.

—DOUG LARSON
CARTOONIST OF "THE FAR SIDE"

I am not against golf, since I cannot but suspect it keeps armies of the unworthy from discovering trout.

—PAUL O'NEILL, FISHING FANATIC

Scholars have long known that fishing eventually turns men into philosophers. Unfortunately, it is almost impossible to buy decent tackle on a philosopher's salary.

—PATRICK F. McMANUS
FISHING HUMORIST

When a whopper bass pops your line at the knot, nothing says "you're a knothead" so eloquently as that little curl where the knot unraveled.

—HOMER CIRCLE
   **A.K.A. "UNCLE HOMER,"
   BASS EXPERT,
   FROM** *BASS WISDOM*

All the romance of trout fishing exists in the mind of the angler and is in no way shared by the fish.

—HAROLD F. BLAISDELL
FROM *THE PHILOSOPHICAL FISHERMAN*

The river was tougher than a $2 steak.

There is a rich expectancy in the act of packing for a fishing trip. Some people spend the last hours in military fervor, with their gear in neat piles and a checklist in hand, as exacting as Douglas MacArthur on the eve of a campaign, but I tend to be cavalier and abide by a single rule: I make sure to pack my rod and reel.

—BILL BARICH
CRAZY FOR RIVERS

Fish and visitors smell in
three days.

—BENJAMIN FRANKLIN
SCIENTIST, INVENTOR, STATESMAN,
PRINTER, PHILOSOPHER, MUSICIAN
AND ECONOMIST

Even if you've been fishing for three hours and haven't gotten anything except poison ivy and sunburn, you're still better off than the worm.

—ANONYMOUS

May the holes in your net be no larger than the fish in it.

—IRISH BLESSING

If you've got short, stubby fingers and wear reading glasses, any relaxation you would normally derive from fly fishing is completely eliminated when you try to tie on a fly.

—JACK OHMAN
POLITICAL CARTOONIST

[B]ecause no man is born an artist, so no man is born an angler.

—IZAAK WALTON
**"GRAND-PÈRE" OF
FISHING WRITERS, FROM**
THE COMPLEAT ANGLER

"Carpe Diem" does not mean "fish of the day."

—ANONYMOUS

Anticipation is such a pleasurable part of fly fishing that it sometimes seems a shame to go out someplace, cast, and try to catch something.

—SETH NORMAN
*THE FLY FISHER'S GUIDE
TO CRIMES OF PASSION*

Zen and the art of ice
fishing is an oxymoron.

—ANONYMOUS

A peasant between two lawyers
is like a fish between two cats.

—SPANISH PROVERB

You think six pounds a day will win the Classic? Think again.

—MIKE IACONELLI

ON HIS POOR LUCK IN THE EARLY ROUNDS OF THE 2003 CITGO BASSMASTER CLASSIC CHAMPIONSHIP IN NEW ORLEANS, THAT HE EVENTUALLY WENT ON TO WIN

I took the old reel apart to learn its secrets, then

I put a new reel on the rod and filled it with line,

discovering every tangle trial and error can pro-

duce. It's a task that requires four hands, and I

had to make do with two and a pair of knees.

—LEANNE SCHREIBER
"MIDSTREAM," FROM *MIDSTREAM*

Most Western Native American tribes had a saying about grizzly tracks—about fishing or hunting someplace else when you found them. A few weeks ago I came around a bend on a mountain trail in the Bob Marshall Wilderness and found myself within sixty feet of a boar grizzly. I didn't recall any Indian sayings at the time, but the idea of fishing someplace else suddenly made a lot of sense.

—JOHN BARSNESS
FIELD & STREAM AUTHOR,
"A TROUT STREAM NAMED DESIRE,"
FROM *MONTANA TIME*

What light from yonder lakefront burns?

Is it our fair sun come arisen on morning hillcrest?

No, it is the bobber.

—CHRISTOPHER ARELT
   (ONE OF THE
   "BROWN WATER BOYS"),
   "ODE TO THE BOBBER,"
   FROM *THE OFFBEAT ANGLER*

Many fishermen think trout are color-blind, but that is nothing to what trout think of fishermen.

—ED ZERN

**FIELD & STREAM WRITER
AND FISHING HUMORIST,
"A CREELFUL OF ZERN"
FROM** *HUNTING AND FISHING
A TO ZERN*

A fly-fishing Nazi is someone who believes there is only one way to fish properly, and that is with artificial flies. The worst kind of elitists, they consider any other approach to fishing unacceptable, and strongly suggestive of questionable paternity and a room-temperature IQ.

—PAUL QUINNETT
NATIONALLY KNOWN
PSYCHOLOGIST, AUTHOR,
FISHING HUMORIST,
FROM *FISHING LESSONS*

Fishing is boring unless you catch an actual fish, and then it is disgusting.

—DAVE BARRY
HUMORIST

People who fish for food, and sport be damned, are called pot-fishermen. The more expert ones are called crack pot-fishermen. All other fishermen are called crackpot fishermen. This is confusing.

—ED ZERN
FISHING HUMORIST

Cape Cod kids don't use no sleds

Haul away, heave away

They slide down hills on codfish heads

—SEA CHANTEY

I mean, man alive, me on TV is like pourin' perfume on a pig.

—BILL DANCE

ON HIS FIRST SHOOT OF THE PROGRAM *BILL DANCE OUTDOORS*, QUOTED IN *THE FISHING CLUB* BY BOB RICH

'Twas the night before fishing

When all through the house

Lay Dad's scattered fishing gear

As though strewn by a souse. . . .

'Twas the morning after the first day

When all through the house

Echoed the moaning and groaning

Of poor daddy—the louse!

—ROBERT TRAVER
**NOM DE PLUME OF
JOHN VOELKER,
FROM** *TROUT MADNESS*

When four fishermen get to-gether, there's always a fifth.

—SPENCER APOLLONIO
FORMER HEAD OF
THE MAINE DEPARTMENT
OF MARINE RESOURCES

A visit to a first-class fishing-tackle shop is more interesting than an afternoon at the circus.

—THEODORE GORDON
INVENTOR OF THE QUILL GORDON,
ONE OF THE FIRST AMERICAN
DRY FLIES

What a tourist terms a plague of insects, the fly fisher calls a great hatch.

—PATRICK F. McMANUS
FISHING HUMORIST

Much is made of logic in fly-fishing these days, especially when it comes to trout, but the bass-fisherman is still often faced with trying to decide whether his fish will eat a red and white thing as opposed to a bright yellow thing when there's no discernible reason why he should bite either.

—JOHN GIERACH
"MUSIC OF THE SPHERES," FROM
THE VIEW FROM RAT LAKE

The fishing was good, it was the catching that was bad.

—A. K. BEST

**WORLD-FAMOUS FLY TIER AND
AUTHOR OF FLY TYING BOOKS**

FISHING
SAGES

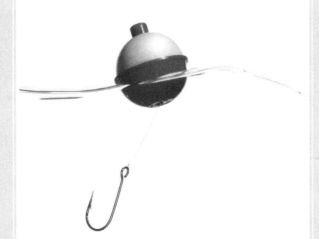

Sir, this pleasant curiosity of fish and fishing . . . has been thought worthy of the *pens and practices* of divers in other nations, that have been reputed men of great *learning and wisdom.* . . .

—IZAAK WALTON
"GRAND-PÈRE"
OF FISHING WRITERS,
FROM *THE COMPLEAT ANGLER*

Time is probably more generous to an angler than to any other individual.

—ZANE GREY
"THE FIRST THOUSAND-POUNDER,"
FROM *ZANE GREY: OUTDOORSMAN*

Fishing is a . . . discipline in the equality of men—for all men are equal before fish.

—HERBERT HOOVER
FISHERMAN AND 31ST PRESIDENT
OF THE UNITED STATES

Many men go fishing all of their lives without knowing that it is not fish they are after.

—HENRY DAVID THOREAU
AMERICAN AUTHOR,
NATURALIST, TRANSCENDENTALIST,
TAX RESISTER

Anglers must always face the fish alone, and that is how it should be.

—STEVE RAYMOND
RIVERS OF THE HEART

Wind northeast,

Fish bite least,

Wind southwest,

Fish bite best.

—NEW ENGLAND SAYING

When the wind is in the east,

Then the fishes bite the least;

When the wind is in the west,

Then the fishes bite the best;

When the wind is in the north

Then the fishes do come forth

When the wind is in the south,

It blows the bait in the fish's mouth.

—ANONYMOUS

No human being, however great, or powerful, was so free as a fish.

—JOHN RUSKIN
ART CRITIC, POET, ARTIST, AND
AUTHOR OF *THE TWO PATHS*

It is not a fish until it is on the bank.

—IRISH PROVERB

Beauty without grace is the hook without the bait.

—RALPH WALDO EMERSON
AMERICAN AUTHOR,
POET, PHILOSOPHER

If you wish to be happy for an hour,
get intoxicated.

If you wish to be happy for three days,
get married.

If you wish to be happy for eight days,
kill your pig and eat it.

If you wish to be happy forever,
learn to fish.

—CHINESE PROVERB

How like fish we are: ready, nay eager, to seize upon whatever new thing some wind of circumstance shakes down upon the river of time! And how we rue our haste, finding the gilded morsel to contain a hook.

—ALDO LEOPOLD

A SAND COUNTY ALMANAC

For the supreme test of a fisherman
is not how many fish he has caught,
not even how he has caught them,
but what he has caught when he has
caught no fish.

—JOHN H. BRADLEY,
FISHERMAN

Time is money, and trout are not money. You can buy them or earn them, but not spend them.

—JOHN BARSNESS
FIELD & STREAM **AUTHOR,**
"A TROUT STREAM NAMED DESIRE"
FROM *MONTANA TIME*

A fisherman once stung
will be wiser.

—LATIN PROVERB

There will be days when the fishing is better than one's most optimistic forecast, others when it is far worse. Either is a gain over just staying home.

—RODERICK HAIG-BROWN
WRITER, MAGISTRATE, PIONEER
CONSERVATIONIST, FISHERMAN

These brook trout will strike any fly you present, provided you don't get close enough to present it.

—DICK BLALOCK
FORMER U.S. FOREIGN SERVICE
OFFICER, COLLEGE FOOTBALL
PLAYER, FISHERMAN

Fishing is mostly tough luck. "The big ones get away" is its basic slogan. And the bigger the fish the angler seeks, the tougher his misfortune is likely to be.

—PHILIP WYLIE
"LISTEN TO THIS TALE OF WOE,"
FROM *A TREASURY OF TRUE*

The more we fish, the more weight-lessly and quietly we move through a river and among its fish, and the more we resemble our own minds in the bliss of angling.

—THOMAS McGUANE
FROM *THE LONGEST SILENCE*

Fishing is cumulative, though you don't learn all of it, ever.

—NICK LYONS
FROM *BRIGHT RIVERS*

FISHING
FOOLS

Rivers and the inhabitants of the watery elements are made for wise men to contemplate and for fools to pass without consideration.

—IZAAK WALTON
"GRAND-PERE" OF
FISHING WRITERS, FROM
THE COMPLEAT ANGLER

As the years had passed I had observed that for every catch which won a prize there were uncountable tales of disaster, ignominy and rugged misfortune.

—PHILIP WYLIE
ON THE CREATION OF
THE "PHILIP WYLIE HARD LUCK
TROPHY" FOR VARIOUS FLORIDA
FISHING TOURNAMENTS,
"LISTEN TO THIS TALE OF WOE,"
FROM *A TREASURY OF TRUE*

I love sports and I wanted to do something competitively one more time before I was a goddamned geriatric. God, when you're in your 40s, what sports are left? Fishing?

—MICKEY ROURKE
**ACTOR, PERHAPS NOT
A FISHING FANATIC**

The Upper Dam at Rangeley [Lake, Maine] is the place, of all others in the world, where the lunacy of angling may be seen in its incurable stage.

—HENRY VAN DYKE

"A FATAL SUCCESS"

There's a fine line between fishing and standing on shore like an idiot.

—STEPHEN WRIGHT
COMEDIAN

Fly fishing may be a very pleasant
amusement; but angling or float fishing
I can only compare to a stick and a
string, with a worm at one end and
a fool at the other.

—SAMUEL JOHNSON
**POET, ESSAYIST, BIOGRAPHER,
LEXICOGRAPHER**

The calamities that may befall an angler who whips a brook trout are fairly limited. He can, to be sure, fall into a deep pool and drown; he can step on a rattlesnake or in a hornet's nest; he can concentrate so hard on a fighting trout that he fails to evade a bull charging across a pasture. But when a man takes himself out to sea with vastly heavier gear, he greatly increases the likelihood of misfortune even though he is reasonably safe from bulls, hornets and serpents.

—PHILIP WYLIE
"LISTEN TO THIS TALE OF WOE,"
A TREASURY OF TRUE

It has always been my private conviction that any man who pits his intelligence against a fish and loses has it coming.

—JOHN STEINBECK
AMERICAN AUTHOR

It is to be observed that "angling" is the name given to fishing by people who can't fish.

—STEPHEN LEACOCK
CANADIAN HUMORIST
AND EDUCATOR

About ninety in a hundred fancy themselves angler. About one in a hundred
is an angler. About ten in a hundred
throw the hatchet better than the fly.

—COLONEL PETER HAWKER
FROM *THE DIARY OF*
COLONEL PETER HAWKER

There he stands, draped in more equipment than a telephone lineman, trying to outwit an organism with a brain no bigger than a breadcrumb, and getting licked in the process.

—PAUL O'NEIL,
ANGLER, FISHING WIT

Even the best bass fishermen have days when they feel bass are finning their noses at them.

—HOMER CIRCLE
(A.K.A. "UNCLE HOMER"),
BASS EXPERT,
FROM *BASS WISDOM*

You see it all the time: fishermen flailing away constantly all day long and complaining in the bar they never catch any fish, like maybe they thought fish lived up in the air because that's where their flies were.

—DAVE AMES
FROM *A GOOD LIFE WASTED*

The awkward fisherman does nothing but disturb the water.

—ANONYMOUS

The sport of angling used to be a genteel business, at least in the world of ideals, a world of ladies and gentlemen. These have been replaced by a new set of paradigms: the bum, the addict, and the maniac.

—THOMAS McGUANE
FROM *THE LONGEST SILENCE*

[N]ot everything about fishing

is noble, reasonable and sane. . . .

—HENRY MIDDLETON

RIVERS OF MEMORY

There is nothing so pathetic as a small-stream trout specialist on a tough bone-fish flat.

—JAMES BABB
EDITOR OF *GRAY'S SPORTING JOURNAL*, FROM *A FLY FISHER'S FOUR SEASONS*

There out there tearin' their underwear an' bruisin' their legs and they look like a monkey hoein' cabbage.

—LEFTY KREH

ON HOW SOME FLY FISHERMEN LOOK DOING THE DOUBLE HAUL CAST, FROM *FLY CASTING WITH LEFTY KREH*

A
CREELFUL
OF QUOTES

A monk in his cloister, a fish in the water, a thief in the gallows.

—GERMAN PROVERB

Often I have been exhausted on trout streams, uncomfortable, wet, cold, briar scarred, sunburned, mosquito bitten, but never with a fly rod in my hand have I been less than in a place that was less than beautiful.

—CHARLES KURALT
NEWSMAN, FISHERMAN

The true fisherman approaches the first day of fishing season with all the wonder and awe of a child approaching Christmas.

—ROBERT TRAVER
NOM DE PLUME OF JOHN VOELKER,
RETIRED MICHIGAN SUPREME
COURT JUSTICE AND FISHERMAN

Bimini was a place where you could pull in fish forever, where you could troll and never grow old, where your father would never die.

—FRED WAITZKIN
FROM *THE LAST MARLIN*

Perhaps the simple rhythms of life sustained our family during those Great Depression years, and bass fishing became part of our family rituals. . . .

—ERNEST SCHWIEBERT
"THOUGHTS IN COLTSFOOT TIME,"
FROM *DEATH OF A RIVERKEEPER*

When I think of home, I think of fishing with my dad. We'd go to a sandpit loaded with bluegill and bullheads.

—MARG HELGENBERGER

ACTRESS, FISHERWOMAN

What we gain in hake,
we lose in herring.

—ENGLISH PROVERB

The worst part of losing good fish is that you cannot release them. They tailwalk across the back of your mind for days.

—CHRISTOPHER CAMUTO
AUTHOR OF *A FLY FISHERMAN'S BLUE RIDGE*

Once fishing was a rabbit's foot—

O wind blow cold, O wind blow hot

—ROBERT LOWELL
AMERICAN POET

We fished not until the light had failed but until we were sore-armed from casting and tired of catching trout. As we walked away from the river, I thought I must have crossed over into the realm of the eternally fortunate and would have such days forever, but I was mistaken. It was only our turn to be rewarded.

—BILL BARICH
CRAZY FOR RIVERS

About this time the natives again sighted sharks coming around the boat. I did not like this. Uncanny devils!

—ZANE GREY
DESCRIBING HIS FIGHT WITH
A 1,250-POUND BLUE MARLIN,
"THE FIRST THOUSAND-POUNDER,"
FROM *ZANE GREY: OUTDOORSMAN*

I have other fish to fry.

—MIGUEL DE CERVANTES
SPANISH AUTHOR

Lots of images come to mind when people think about nuclear power. Jane Fonda . . . Hazardous waste . . . Chernobyl. Three Mile Island. Great fishing.

—SEBASTIAN O'KELLY
ONE OF THE "BROWN WATER BOYS," FROM *THE OFFBEAT ANGLER*

Now why should Lefty Kreh presume to tell you where to fish?

—LEFTY KREH
LEFTY'S FAVORITE
FLY-FISHING WATERS

I like fishing locally. I *insist* on fishing locally.

—WILLIAM TAPPLY
GONE FISHIN'

[B]y the time I turned sixteen . . . I thought that
sitting in a boat in the middle of nowhere was the
dumbest activity known to mankind and swore I
would never fish again—and I might have kept my
promise, too, if my brother hadn't intervened by
accident, thirteen years later.

—BILL BARICH
FROM *CRAZY FOR RIVERS*

Normally I'm from the bigger-is-better school of thought, but there will forever remain the debate: would you rather catch six 12-inch fish or one 18-inch in a one-hour period?

—CHRISTOPHER ARELT
ONE OF THE "BROWN
WATER BOYS," FROM
THE OFFBEAT ANGLER

The contentment which fills the mind of the angler at the close of his day's sport is one of the chiefest charms in his life.

—WILLIAM COWPER PRIME
AUTHOR, NEWSPAPERMAN,
AND PRESIDENT OF
THE ASSOCIATED PRESS

He seems to regard angling as an amusement in which to pass the time pleasantly, rather than as a craft to be closely studied.

—W. EARL HODGSON
PROLIFIC ANGLING AUTHOR

Men lived like fishes; the great ones devour'd the small.

—ALGERNON SIDNEY
17TH-CENTURY AUTHOR,
INSPIRATION FOR
THE AMERICAN REVOLUTION

The day was fine—not another
hook in the brook.

—DANIEL WEBSTER
PROMINENT AMERICAN STATESMAN
AND NATURALIST

No human activity other than sex and murder has spawned more books than fishing.

—WILLIAM TAPPLY
GONE FISHIN'

When I go fishing I like to know that there's nobody within five miles of me.

—NORMAN MacCAIG

SCOTTISH POET AND FISHERMAN

I can think of nobody who has written about

angling more beautifully than Odell Shepard,

at least since [Izaak] Walton.

—ARNOLD GINGRICH
FOUNDER OF *ESQUIRE* MAGAZINE,
FISHERMAN, QUOTED
BY LAMAR UNDERWOOD IN
*THE GREATEST FISHING STORIES
EVER TOLD*

Bill Dance has literally become an industry himself and yet through it all, he has retained the humility and trademark self-deprecating humor that have made him an American icon.

—BOB RICH
ON PERHAPS THE SINGLE
BEST-KNOWN FISHERMAN IN
AMERICAN FISHING,
FROM *THE FISHING CLUB*

I suspect that . . . many of those worthy gentlemen who are given to haunt the sides of pastoral streams with angle rods in hand, may trace the origin of their passion to the seductive pages of honest Izaak Walton.

—WASHINGTON IRVING
"THE ANGLER"

Beware of taking to collect books on angling. You will find yourself become so attached to the fascinating hobby, that you would pawn the shirt off your back to obtain some coveted edition.

—R. B. MARSTON

LEGENDARY AND MOST ESTEEMED ANGLER AND EDITOR OF THE *FISHING GAZETTE*

SELECTED WORKS

Ames, Dave. *True Love and the Woolly Bugger*. The Lyons Press, Guilford, CT, 2004.

——*A Good Life Wasted*. The Lyons Press, Guilford, CT, 2003.

Arelt, Christopher, and Sebastian O'Kelly. *The Offbeat Angler*. Flat Hammock Press, Mystic, CT, 2005.

Babb, James R. *A Fly Fisher's Four Seasons*. The Lyons Press, Guilford, CT, 2001.

Barich, Bill. *Crazy for Rivers*. The Lyons Press, Guilford, CT, 1999.

Bignami, Louis, et al. *Wit & Wisdom of Fishing: Funny Lines & Fishy Advice*. Publications International, Ltd., Lincolnwood, IL, 1998.

Buffler, Rob, and Tom Dickson. *Fishing for Buffalo*. Minneapolis, MN, 1990.

Circle, Homer. *Bass Wisdom*. The Lyons Press, Guilford, CT, 2000.

Goddard, John. *A Fly Fisher's Reflections*. The Lyons Press, Guilford, CT, 2002.

Iaconelli, Mike, with Andrew and Brian Kamenetzky, *Fishing on the Edge*. Delacorte Press, New York, NY, 2005.

Kreh, Lefty. *Fly Casting with Lefty Kreh*. (Video) Tomorrow River Press, Wasau, WI, 1992.

Kreh, Lefty, and Harry Middleton. *Lefty's Favorite Fly-Fishing Waters*. The Lyons Press, Guilford, CT, 2004.

Kurlansky, Mark. *Cod: A Biography of the Fish That Changed the World*. Penguin Books, New York, NY, 1998.

Lyons, Nick. *Bright Rivers*. J. B. Lippincott, New York, NY, 1977.

Lyons, Nick, ed. *Classic Fishing Stories*. The Lyons Press, Guilford, CT, 2002.

Maclean, Norman. *A River Runs Through It*. The University of Chicago Press, Chicago & London, 1976.

McGuane, Thomas. *The Longest Silence: A Life in Fishing*. Alfred A. Knopf Inc., New York, NY, 1999.

McManus, Patrick F. *They Shoot Canoes, Don't They?* Henry Holt and Company, Inc., New York, NY, 1981.

Quinnett, Paul. *Fishing Lessons: Insights, Fun, and Philosophy from a Passionate Angler*. Andrews McMeel Publishing, Kansas City, MO, 1998.

Rich, Bob. *The Fishing Club*. The Lyons Press, Guilford, CT, 2006.

Raines, Howell. *Fly Fishing Through the Midlife Crisis*. William Morrow and Company, Inc., New York, NY, 1993.

Tapply, William G. *Gone Fishin': Ruminations on Fly Fishing*. The Lyons Press, Guilford, CT, 2004.

Underwood, Lamar, ed. *The Greatest Fishing Stories Ever Told*. The Lyons Press, Guilford, CT, 2000.

Waitzkin, Fred. *The Last Marlin: The Story of a Family at Sea*. Penguin Putnam, Inc., New York, NY, 2000.

Walton, Izaak. *The Compleat Angler*. Introduction by Thomas McGuane. The Ecco Press, Hopewell, NJ. 1995.

Wetherell, W. D. *Vermont River*. The Lyons Press, Guilford, CT, 1984.

Wulff, Lee. *Trout on a Fly*. The Lyons Press, Guilford, CT, 1986.

INDEX